TAK

OFF

THE
TAG

TAKING OFF THE TAG

A TRANSITION GUIDE FOR
RETURNED MISSIONARIES

CLARK B. HINCKLEY
KATHLEEN H. HINCKLEY

DESERET
BOOK
SALT LAKE CITY, UTAH

Visit us at DeseretBook.com

Library of Congress Cataloging-in-Publication Data

Hinckley, Clark B., author.
   Taking off the tag : a transition guide for returned missionaries / Clark B. Hinckley, Kathleen H. Hinckley.
      pages cm
   Includes bibliographical references and index.
   ISBN 978-1-62972-045-6 (paperbound)
   1. Mormon missionaries—Conduct of life. 2. Mormons—Conduct of life. 3. Adjustment (Psychology)—Religious aspects—The Church of Jesus Christ of Latter-day Saints. I. Hinckley, Kathleen H., author. II. Title.
   BX8661.H56 2015
   266'.9332—dc23
                                                       2014048811

Printed in the United States of America
Publishers Printing, Salt Lake City, UT

10 9 8 7 6 5 4 3 2 1

We know beyond the shadow of any doubt that the gospel of Jesus Christ is true and the best is yet to come.

ELDER L. TOM PERRY

Contents

Contents

Preface

The idea for this book came to us in the months after we returned home from serving in the Spain Barcelona Mission. We had served together for three years, Clark as mission president and Kathleen as his companion. It was a glorious experience — unquestionably the most remarkable and rewarding three years of our life to date. When our mission was over and we were released, we were glad to again be with family, delighted to personally meet grandchildren who had been born in our absence (four of them), and excited about the next stage of our life. But we were also reminded of something Clark's brother, a former mission president, had said to us before we left: "The fourth year is the hardest."

Between the time we received our call and the time we attended the seminar for new mission presidents at the Missionary Training Center, we received forty pounds of instructional material. Three years later, we received a single-page letter extending a release and expressing thanks for our service. This pattern is true for all missionaries: there is a vast amount of literature and instructional material to help elders and sisters prepare for missionary service but very little available to guide recently returned missionaries through the transition to postmission life.

As we met with and renewed our relationship with many of our former missionaries who had returned home before us or who returned home in that "fourth year" of our mission, we began to realize that returning home from a full-time mission can be difficult and challenging for many missionaries. We had many conversations with recently returned missionaries and began to see some trends.

This book grew out of those conversations. We began a series of interviews with returned missionaries, conducted a survey of a number of missionaries, and corresponded with others. This book was made possible by their input. While there were too many contributors to name them individually, the ideas of many of them (and quotations from some of them) are found in this book. We are extremely grateful for their input, their candor, and their wisdom.

We also acknowledge the input and ideas we received from several stake presidents and former mission presidents. In one meeting with some returned missionaries, a returned elder mentioned a letter of instruction that he'd been given by his stake president upon his return. We are grateful to President Howard K. Bangerter of the Highland Utah East Stake for sharing with us his wise counsel to returned missionaries in his stake. John Chipman, who pre-sided over the Peru Piura Mission, and his wife, Karen, read an early draft of the manuscript and made several sugges-tions that greatly improved it. Dan Paxton, a good friend and a great teacher, shared his insight on the parameters of a successful transition and other issues facing recently re-turned missionaries. Several recently returned missionaries read various versions of the manuscript and provided im-portant feedback.

Finally, we express thanks and appreciation to our six children and their spouses. Eight of them served missions; all of them married in the temple and continue to keep their covenants as they move through various stages of life. They are an inspiration to us.

The Best Is Yet to Come

Onward, ever onward, as we glory in his name.
Hymns, no. 249

We had been in the mission only a week when the mission secretary brought a stack of letters into Clark's office and asked him to sign them. The secretary explained that they were the "death letters" for missionaries who would be released in three months.

Death letters? We soon learned that there was a rich culture of death surrounding the completion of missionary service: we sang for the "dead," junior companions "killed" their senior companions, missionaries could name the city or ward where returned missionaries had "died." Sometimes districts even held mock funerals for departing missionaries.

Language is powerful. How we talk about events shapes how we feel about those events, and our feelings influence our actions and behaviors, even our success or failure. We had served for only a couple of weeks when Clark interviewed a group of missionaries the day before they returned home. During those interviews he realized how the language of death affected those returning missionaries. They had served well, they had worked hard, they had been obedient, they had learned the power of obedience, and they had performed miracles. They had developed skills and habits that would lead them to great success in life. Yet what Clark discovered during those interviews was that these missionaries—most of them just twenty-one years old—felt that the best of their life was over.

It became clear during the course of those interviews that these missionaries had been told over and over again in countless ways that their mission would be the best two years of their life. *The best two years.* For as long as they could remember, they had heard returned missionaries speak of their mission as the best two years. They had even seen the movie. And they now believed that the best two years of their life were over.

But no one had ever told them that the phrase was incomplete: the complete phrase is, "the best two years *so far!*" We realized that an important part of our calling was to help departing missionaries understand that the best was yet to come.

Changed in the "Twinkling of an Eye"

Missionaries don't "die" when they go home. Instead, they experience a transition much more glorious—they are changed in the twinkling of an eye.

And it happens that fast. One moment you are a full-time

missionary, sure of your purpose, confident in your calling, with an eye single to the glory of God. The next instant you are, well, something different: a returned missionary.

The Doctrine and Covenants states that in the Millennium, men "shall not sleep in the dust, but they shall be changed in the twinkling of an eye" (D&C 63:51). Postmission life is not the dust-bowl of mortality; it is something glorious and desirable. Doctrine and Covenants 101:31 adds that in those millennial days a man, rather than dying, will "be changed in the twinkling of an eye, and shall be caught up, and his rest shall be glorious."

We like to paraphrase that verse, changing it ever so slightly as it applies to returning missionaries (who don't get much rest when they return): they "shall be changed in the twinkling of an eye . . . and *the* rest shall be glorious" — the rest of your life and the rest of eternity.

In the scriptures, the phrase "twinkling of an eye" refers to the transition from "mortality to immortality" (3 Nephi 28:8). For a missionary returning home, it refers to leaving the "mortality" of a mission (you knew from the beginning it was limited to eighteen or twenty-four months), to the "immortality" of the rest of your life and all eternity. It is a glorious event, not a death but the beginning of a new and wonderful adventure full of excitement, promise, and happiness.

As a stake president, Clark extended releases to scores of missionaries. Very often, the missionary and his or her family would stop at our home on their way home from the airport. As we opened the door, we could almost see a glow around those returning missionaries. After one such experience, Kathleen remarked, "It's like bringing a new-born home from the hospital. They still have that glow of heaven in their countenance."

Our hope is that this book will help you keep that glow and continue to experience the excitement of miracles, the satisfaction of personal growth, and the tender mercies of the Spirit for the next two years, the two years after that, and throughout your life.

How to Use This Book

This book is designed to assist you in your transition from being a full-time missionary to being a full-time Latter-day Saint. It will help you bring some structure and direction into your life in the absence of the structure and direction of missionary life. It is not the "white handbook" of postmission life—because postmission life is much more varied than the life of a full-time missionary, there is no single fifty-page handbook that will guide you—but it will help you write your own personal handbook and revise your handbook as your life moves forward.

This book includes observations and advice from more than fifty returned missionaries. There was widespread agreement among these missionaries on most issues, but each of them had unique experiences during their transition. Your experience as a returned missionary will be different from the experiences of your companions, friends, or family members, but you will probably identify with much of what they say.

We love missionaries and returned missionaries and

hope that this book will help you think about important issues, ask the right questions, and begin to find some answers. Like *Preach My Gospel*, it has information boxes with scripture references and suggested activities. These activities are the most valuable part of this book. They will help you study, ponder, pray, and receive divine direction. As you read this book, you may want to have a study journal handy to take notes and to record the activities.

As a missionary, you spent at least two hours every morning studying and planning. If you will devote a portion of your morning study time now to this book and the activities it contains, you will be able to complete most of them within a few weeks.

This book draws heavily upon *Preach My Gospel*. With its succinct summaries of restored truth in chapter 3, as well as chapters devoted to how to study effectively, how to recognize and understand the Spirit, how to understand the role of the Book of Mormon, how to develop Christlike attributes, and how to use time wisely, *Preach My Gospel* can continue to be a valuable resource in your life. It is no wonder that Elder Richard G. Scott of the Quorum of the Twelve Apostles observed, "The best is yet to come as we all become more proficient in the use of this extraordinary missionary tool."[1]

This book also contains QR codes that link to expanded materials on the Internet. If you have a smartphone, you can access those links using any QR reader application.

You may have received counsel from your mission president before your release or from a priesthood leader since arriving home that conflicts with some of the advice in this book. If there is such a conflict, follow the counsel of your priesthood leaders. They know you, they know your specific situation, and they give inspired counsel. Obtain your own spiritual confirmation of their counsel through the Holy Ghost. As you follow their inspired counsel, you will be blessed.

You will be a returned missionary for the rest of your life. Your mission changed you, and we hope this book will help you to continue changing, improving, and growing, much as you did during the past eighteen or twenty-four months. Making the right choices over the next few weeks, months, and years will ensure that the Lord's investment in you will be magnified many times over.

Elder L. Tom Perry of the Quorum of the Twelve has given us this invitation and promise:

"I call on you returned missionaries to rededicate yourselves, to become re-infused with the desire and spirit of missionary service. I call on you to look the part, to be the part, and to act the part of a servant of our Father in Heaven. I pray for your renewed determination to proclaim the gospel that you may become more actively engaged in this great work the Lord has called all of us to do. I want to promise you there are great blessings in store for you if you continue to press forward with the zeal you once possessed as a full-time missionary."[2]

Welcome home! The best is yet to come!

1

A Successful Transition

To choose in righteousness
The better part.
Hymns, no. 24

Joshua urged the Israelites, "Choose you this day whom ye will serve" (Joshua 24:15). The choices you make and the actions you take during the first days, weeks, and months after your return home have long-term consequences for you, for your family, for your friends, and for children yet unborn. The lives of two missionaries illustrate the importance of these decisions.

In 1933, two young men from Salt Lake City were called to serve in the British Mission. Both of them came from prominent families, were active in the Church, and had a strong pioneer heritage. In those days of the Great Depression, not many young men received mission calls; both of these new missionaries had already shown signs of greatness — they were talented, educated, and came from families with a heritage of faith and a tradition of success. They served together ably and effectively in England and returned home in 1935.

One of these recently returned missionaries began to drift slowly from full activity in the Church. He was bright, well educated, had lived abroad for two years, and knew something of the world outside his small community. He began to date a young woman who was not a member of the Church. They fell in love and were married. She was active in her own faith, and he accompanied her to her church services when he attended at all. They led good lives. They had children, were active in the community, and were good neighbors, and he was successful in business. But they never obtained the blessings of the sealing ordinance, never had the joy of serving a mission together, never experienced the quiet miracles that come from a lifetime of service in the kingdom of God.

The second returned missionary determined before he came home that he was going to make a difference in the world. When he arrived home, he immediately became involved in his ward and stake. He had learned on his mission to be an effective public speaker, and as a young single adult he was called to serve on the General Sunday School Board. He married his sweetheart in the Salt Lake Temple. They raised five children together while serving actively in the Church and in the community. He served as a counselor in a stake presidency and later as a stake president. At age fifty-one he was ordained an apostle. In 1995, Gordon B. Hinckley was set apart as the fifteenth president of the Church of Jesus Christ of Latter-day Saints.

Both President Hinckley and his missionary companion had been faithful, obedient missionaries. But the decisions they made in those early weeks and months after their return home set them on very different paths.

The decisions you make and the actions you take in your first few months home will put you on a path that becomes progressively more difficult to abandon. Over the next few years you will make decisions that will shape the rest of your life: what you will study, how much education you will receive, whom you will marry, when you will have children, how you will support yourself and your family, where you will establish your home. You will make more important decisions during the next few years than during any comparable period of time in your life. Your mission provided you a foundation as you enter these decisive few years. Your challenge is to use that foundation as a launch pad to move forward and obtain the blessings that await you.

> *You will make more important decisions during the next few years than during any comparable period of time in your life.*

ACTIVITY

List in your study journal some of the important decisions you will make over the next few years. What decisions and actions do you need to take during the next few weeks that will keep you on course to make good decisions in the years that follow? Record your impressions in your study journal.

What Is a Successful Transition?

A successful transition home from full-time missionary service essentially means that your commitment to live the gospel of Jesus Christ continues uninterrupted. You can measure your success along many parameters:

- Your personal religious practices — how frequently and effectively you engage in gospel study, temple attendance, and prayer; how diligent you are in fulfilling your Church calling; and the degree to which obedience has become a continuing quest.

- Your relationships with others — the degree to which you develop healthy and fulfilling relationships with family, friends, ward members, spouse or potential spouse, Church leaders, colleagues at work and/or school, and people with whom you can share the gospel.

- Your engagement in service — the degree to which you continually look for individuals and families whom you can serve and render quiet and meaningful service.

- Your education — how diligently you work to achieve meaningful education goals that prepare you for a career and for greater service in the Church, as well as your commitment to lifelong learning.

- Your work — your progress in finding and doing meaningful work that will enable you to become self-reliant.

- Your physical and emotional health — your efforts to keep your mind and body healthy through proper nutrition, proper physical and mental activity, and sufficient rest and to obtain professional care when needed.

- Your use of leisure time — the degree to which you engage in positive, uplifting activities both individually and with others.

> *"Yea, come unto Christ, and be perfected in him, and deny yourselves of all ungodliness." — Moroni 10:32*

A successful returned missionary is a returned missionary who continues to serve others unselfishly, who makes and keeps covenants, and who strives to become perfected in Christ.

REMEMBER THIS

1. You will make more important decisions during the next few years than during any comparable period of time in your life.

2. Success is measured by the degree to which you serve others, keep your covenants, and strive to become more Christlike.

2

Is It "A Hard Thing"?

You can live a happy life
In this world of toil and strife.
Hymns, no. 228

You probably remember the moment: you had your release interview with your stake president and then, either during that interview or immediately afterward, you carefully removed your missionary name tag. For many missionaries, it is the hardest moment of their entire mission. For all missionaries, taking off the name tag represents a major life change.

But it wasn't the first major life change of the past two years. The moment you put on your name tag, your life changed dramatically. You gave up movies, television, time with friends, time with family, your phone, your music, your free time. Even your ability to email family and friends was restricted. Your daily schedule changed, and your routine changed. When you left the Missionary Training Center and entered the mission, your friends and your living conditions changed again. You may have experienced changes in climate, clothing, food, and language. And for many missionaries, those changes were difficult—not everyone likes chicken feet in their soup, constant rejection, and working outside all day under a blazing sun or in the freezing cold. Missions are hard.

Coming home from a mission has its own set of challenges. The highly structured schedule of mission life disappears, the sense of intense engagement is gone, the constant focus on others shifts. You are likely to experience some or all of the following challenges described by other returned missionaries:

"I just felt awkward."

"I think just feeling out of place was the big fact that made it hard on me."

"I had changed much more than my family or friends had changed. I just wasn't interested in the same things anymore."

"When I was a missionary, my focus was always on serving others—my companion, investigators, members, strangers in the street. Now it seemed all the focus was on me—my education, my financial well-being, my social life."

"Sundays were the hardest. As a missionary, I had found Sunday was the most intense day of the week. Now all I had to do was show up for my meetings."

"What was hard for me was that I felt lazy. I had been going, going, going for two years. Then all of a sudden I am home and have a lot of time for things but I'm not super busy."

"Everyone who knew and loved me wanted to see me,

spend time with me, hear about the mission, pester me about who I would start dating, and though they had good intentions, I felt like they had no idea of the gravity of what had happened to me on the mission, so everything felt trivial and mundane."

"I found myself juggling to work twenty-plus hours a week at the MTC and serve ninety sisters in the Relief Society while carrying a full academic load and applying for graduate schools. I also expected myself to exercise daily, attend the temple weekly, and participate in family history work. I felt joy in service, but I was also sleep deprived and stretched thin." — A returned sister

"What I found most challenging about returning home was dating."

"The most difficult challenge for me was figuring out how to stay close to the Lord while living a 'normal' life."

"My friends wanted to show me everything I had missed while I was gone, but I really didn't want to see or hear about movies, music, or the missteps of former teen stars."

"One of the hardest things for me was the expectations of others. Everyone wanted to know what my plans were, what I was going to study, if I was dating, when I was getting married!"

"I missed the mantle of the calling, the sense of purpose associated with that mantle, and the constant spiritual guidance that accompanied it."

The list goes on and on. You may feel fear of the unknown future. You may find the sudden lack of structure and schedule somewhat alarming. Even for missionaries who quickly become involved in work, school, dating, and Church callings, the task of juggling so many different aspects of life can be overwhelming.

As a returned missionary, you are accustomed to doing hard things. Missionary life is hard. The schedule is demanding. Companions can be difficult. Disappointment and rejection are common. Learning a foreign language is frustrating. People who don't keep their commitments are frustrating. Spending the day walking around in rain, snow, or blistering heat while wearing your Sunday best can be miserable. If you served an honorable and faithful mission, you can do just about anything.

> *"Don't think you can't be happy." – A returned missionary*

But one of the reasons your mission was the best eighteen months or two years so far is that it was harder than any previous time in your life. And the challenges you experience during the next few years will, in the same way, make these years both memorable and valuable.

Nephi and his brothers were living a comfortable life in their home near Jerusalem, enjoying all that money could buy. Then suddenly they were living in tents in the wilderness. When Lehi asked them to return to Jerusalem to obtain the brass plates from Laban, it was too much for Laman and Lemuel. They complained "it is a hard thing" that Lehi required of them. But Nephi had a different perspective: he simply said, "I will go and do the things which the Lord hath commanded" (1 Nephi 3:5, 7). The challenges and difficulties of their trip back to Jerusalem and their encounters with Laban were, in fact, "a hard thing" for Laman and Lemuel, including a stern reprimand from an angel. But for Nephi the same challenges and difficulties were filled with spiritual manifestations and a great strengthening of his faith.

ACTIVITY

Read 1 Nephi 2:15–16, 1 Nephi 3–4.

List the challenges faced by Nephi. Why did Nephi respond to these challenges differently from Laman and Lemuel?

Does Attitude Affect Outcome?

Nephi and his brothers were all subjected to the same set of changes in their life: leaving their comfortable home to live in a tent in the wilderness, traveling back to Jerusalem to obtain the brass plates from a recalcitrant Laban who would rather kill them than give them the plates, giving up their inheritance, building a ship with no previous ship-building experience, and crossing an unknown ocean. Yet the identical circumstances resulted in very different personal experiences and outcomes.

In his final interview before returning home, one elder made an interesting observation. During the first year of his mission, he saw only sporadic success in finding, teaching, and baptizing converts. During the second year of his mission, he saw a baptism of a new convert nearly every week. "I don't think I was more obedient during the second year—I had been obedient from the beginning. I was perhaps a better teacher, but not that much better. I didn't work harder—I had been diligent from the beginning. The only thing I can think of is that at the mid-point of my mission I had a companion who helped me understand that it was possible to baptize every week. Once I really knew that was possible, it seemed the Lord constantly put us in contact with people who were amazingly prepared."

Can our attitudes, our beliefs, our faith, actually change the outcomes we experience? It was true for Nephi. It was true for the elder we've just quoted. And scientists suggest it is true for all of us. In a study published in the *Journal of Thoracic Oncology*, researchers examined the survival time of 534 adults diagnosed with lung cancer. All of the patients had completed a personality

> *"My only issue was feeling a little guilty that I didn't struggle at all upon returning home. . . . I would want returning missionaries to know that it isn't guaranteed that you'll struggle. It* is *possible for you to happily jump back into normal life—school, work, relationships—while maintaining the depth you gained as a missionary. You don't need to expect it to be hard. It's just another transfer. Jump into it with enthusiasm and look back only enough to retain the things you learned in the previous area. Life is wonderful!"—A returned sister*

> *"Remember that the mission is a calling, and just like every calling, you get released! You should be excited about this new chapter in your life."*
> — *A returned missionary*

inventory assessment prior to their diagnosis. The study reported that "those having an optimistic explanatory style survived approximately six months longer than patients classified as having a pessimistic explanatory style."[1] The study noted that several previous studies of patients with a variety of diseases had reached similar conclusions: the personal views, perceptions, and expectations of patients had a measurable impact on survival rates.

Not every missionary has a difficult or hard transition upon returning home. If your transition is relatively easy, be grateful. Many missionaries have challenges when they come home — that's how we grow. But the fact is, if you believe that your transition as you return from full-time missionary service will be difficult and that the best eighteen months or two years of your life are over, you are probably right. If you believe that, in spite of challenges and difficulties, the best is yet to come, you are probably right.

Your New Tag

Even though you have removed the plastic name tag that seemed an inseparable part of who you were, you still carry the name of the Savior with you every day. Last Sunday when you partook of the sacrament, you renewed important covenants. One of those was a covenant to take the name of the Savior upon you, to "always remember him and keep his commandments" (D&C 20:77). You still wear His name every day, painted "on your heart—painted, as Paul said, 'not with ink, but with the Spirit of the living God' (2 Corinthians 3:3)."² Carrying His name painted on your heart—every day of every week—reminds you and all who see you of who you are and whom you represent. This, at least, has not changed with your release as a full-time missionary: you still wear a badge identifying you as a representative and disciple of Christ. It is no longer written in plastic nor "in tables of stone, but in fleshy tables of the heart" (2 Corinthians 3:3).

REMEMBER THIS

1. "Hard things" are often the most rewarding.

2. Our expectations and attitudes affect what happens to us.

3. Believe that the best is yet to come!

4. You still wear the Savior's name every day.

3

"Mind the Gap"

And if we are not mindful,
The chance will fade away.
Hymns, no. 226

Riders of the London underground system are familiar with the phrase "Mind the gap." It is on signs in every tube stop (subway station), put there to remind passengers to be careful of the gap between the station platform and the train car. An inattentive subway patron could easily catch his foot in the gap and suffer serious injury. To avoid such injury, passengers are frequently reminded by signs and audio announcements to "mind the gap."

Every returning missionary has a "gap" period—the time between arriving home and beginning school or work. Your gap may be only a few days, or it may be a few months. Regardless of length, it is a precious and valuable time, a brief moment between the single focus of full-time missionary service and the busy and multifaceted next phase of your life. If you "mind the gap," you can use that time to your advantage.

Three Things to Do Now

The first few days at home have some unique challenges. You probably feel awkward. You don't know how to act. People are asking you questions you don't want to answer, and not asking the questions you do want to answer. Don't worry about it. The most important thing you can do this week is ponder about, articulate, and commit to writing some very important thoughts while your mission is still very fresh on your mind.

So before you do anything else, consider doing these three things:

Make a list of things you learned on your mission. Some of these things will be life-changing lessons about prayer, faith, repentance, the Atonement, and the doctrine of Christ. Some of them may be significant skills: how to speak Tagalog (or Texan), how to teach by asking inspired questions, how to really listen. Some of them may be more trivial: the importance of separating darks and lights when doing the wash, how to make a great omelet, how to shower and dress in ten minutes. Start with ten things, then twenty, and keep adding to this list over the next few weeks until you have one hundred items. You will be surprised by how much you have learned during the past eighteen or twenty-four months, and you'll feel grateful for it.

Write your testimony of Jesus Christ and the gospel. Put down on paper how you feel about the Savior, the Atonement, the Church, the plan of salvation. This is for your eyes only, a record of your testimony at the conclusion of your mission. Over the years it will become a valuable document. During a time of difficulty or doubt, it will remind you what you once knew; years from now it may also remind you of how your testimony, faith, and understanding have grown and matured.

Set goals. Make three lists: short-term goals (what you plan to accomplish in the next few weeks); medium-term goals (to be accomplished over the next few months and years); and long-term goals (what you want to accomplish in your life).

> "I am so thoroughly convinced that if we don't set goals in our life and learn how to master the techniques of living to reach our goals, we can reach a ripe old age and look back on our life only to see that we reached but a small part of our full potential."
> — Elder M. Russell Ballard, in Preach My Gospel, 146

The list of short- and medium-term goals you make here will help guide you during the early months of your transition home, while the long-term goals will lift your vision and give you direction. Don't be afraid to think big: this list of long-term goals is your bucket list for life. What do you want to do? What do you want to be? Dream big, and write those dreams down.

Don't worry about getting these lists perfect—you will have frequent opportunities to change and modify your goals, adding new ones and deleting goals that are no longer relevant as you go through your life. These initial lists are just a starting point. In chapter 8 you will spend some time reviewing these goals.

You may already have been home for a while by the time you read this book. That's okay. Complete this exercise now, whether you have been home for a week or a year or longer. But the sooner you do it, the more valuable it will be to you. Why? Not only because it is easier to do this exercise before your life gets busy with school, working, dating, Church service, and a host of other obligations and activities—but because your priorities, outlook, and vision are particularly clear when you return home from your mission.

Cowboy poet Bruce Kiskaddon understood that there are moments in life when we simply have a clearer vision of what is really important:

> Did you ever stand on the ledges,
> On the brink of the great plateau
> And look from their jagged edges
> On the country that lay below?
>
> When your vision met no resistance
> And nothing to stop your gaze,
> Till the mountain peaks in the distance
> Stood wrapped in a purple haze.
>
> While you're gazing on such a vision
> And your outlook is clear and wide,
> If you have to make a decision,
> That's the time and place to decide.

Although you return to the city
And mingle again with the throng;
Though your heart may be softened by pity
Or bitter from strife and wrong.

Though others should laugh in derision,
And the voice of the past grow dim;
Yet, stick to the cool decision
That you made on the mountain's rim.[1]

The completion of your full-time missionary service is one of those times when "your outlook is clear and wide." It is the perfect "time and place to decide." There is no better time in your life to set meaningful goals.

ACTIVITY

- In your study journal, begin to make a list of things you learned on your mission.

- In your study journal, write your testimony.

- Read and review "How to Set Goals," *Preach My Gospel,* 146. How do these principles apply to you in this new phase of your life?

- Prayerfully set some long-term, medium-term, and short-term goals, and write them in your study journal.

Three Things to Remember

"O remember, remember," pleaded Alma to his sons (Alma 37:13). The word *remember* appears more than four hundred times in the scriptures. We keep journals so we can remember. Moroni exhorts us to read the Book of Mormon and "*remember* how merciful the Lord hath been unto the children of men" (Moroni 10:3; emphasis added).

Your missionary experiences will no longer be the center of your life or the subject of every conversation, but it is important to remember them. It is valuable and important to go back occasionally and read your missionary

> "*Many times when I have found myself in difficult times, the Lord has helped me remember situations and events from my mission to help me get through the new difficulties well.*" — *A returned sister*

journal—that's one of the reasons you kept a journal. But there are three things in particular that every returned missionary should always remember:

First, you were a successful missionary. Maybe you wonder if you were the missionary you could have been or should have been. You probably weren't perfect—no missionary is. Nearly every missionary could have been more obedient, more diligent, more faithful, but with very, very few exceptions, every missionary should be proud of the service he or she rendered. If you have any question about how well you served, contact your mission president and ask him. Most important, ask the Lord how He feels about your service. Even President Brigham Young needed to know how the Lord felt about his service, and he was comforted by the Lord's response: "Your offering is acceptable to me" (D&C 126:1). You need to know that your offering was acceptable to the Lord.

 Elder Erich W. Kopischke, "Being Accepted of the Lord," April 2013 general conference, http://www.lds.org/ensign/2013/05 /being-accepted-of-the-lord

Second, you are clean. One of the great promises made to missionaries is found in Doctrine and Covenants 31:5: "Therefore, thrust in your sickle with all your soul, *and your sins are forgiven you*" (emphasis added). If any sin or transgression in your life has not been fully resolved with the appropriate priesthood leaders, you still need to resolve it. But your missionary service assures you of complete forgiveness. Having thrust in your sickle with your might, your sins are forgiven. As you come home from your mission, you are truly beginning a new life, as if you had been born again.

Third, the best is yet to come. The "future is as bright as your faith."[2] The Lord calls young men and women on missions not because they are the best equipped of all His children to preach the gospel to all the world but because He is preparing them for much greater service in the years ahead. Your greatest service in the kingdom and the best years of your life are yet to come.

REMEMBER THIS

1. You were a successful missionary.

2. You are clean.

3. The best is yet to come.

4
Getting Started

Don't stand idly looking on.
Hymns, no. 252

There are several other things you will probably need to do in the first few days you are home. Here are a few thoughts about your other tasks in the first week.

Unpack

Unpacking sounds simple, but every item in your suitcase is filled with memories. Keep handy your journal, your study journals, and any departing advice your mission president gave you—you may want to refer to them from time to time, and they are powerful visual reminders of your experiences. Put your missionary name tag and other souvenirs in an appropriate place. Give your worn-out clothes to Deseret Industries or

> *"Find your old missionary tag. Don't wear it, but put it where you can see it."*
> *— Elder Neil L. Andersen, "It's a Miracle," 78*

Goodwill or someone else who may be able to use them. And while you are unpacking your suitcases, begin to unpack mentally and emotionally. You have arrived in a new "area" — settle in and learn to love it.

Reconnect with Family

You haven't seen each other for many months, and this is a joyful reunion. If you have siblings, consider spending some one-on-one time with each of them to talk, share feelings and experiences, and reconnect.

You may discover that your family members still see you as the person you were when you left, not the person you are now. For you, everything has changed; for your family and friends, almost nothing has changed. You may feel that they are not as diligent in such things as scripture study, family prayers, or family home evening as you think they should be. Be as patient and loving with them as you were with your investigators. Don't tell them what to do; just be a good example and love them in spite of their weaknesses. You will discover over the next few months that they are better than you thought they were!

> "Remember, while you were gone, others may not have grown as much as you did. Do not be disappointed but love them for the growth they have had."
> — A returned sister

Reconnect with Friends

Good friends can be a great support system; the wrong friends can make your life difficult and ultimately pull you onto the wrong track. If you need to, don't hesitate to make new friends that will be part of the kind of support group you need in order to continue to grow and progress in the gospel.

"Everyone needs good and true friends. They will be a great strength and blessing to you. They will influence how you think and act, and even help determine the person you will become. . . . Choose friends who share your values so you can strengthen and encourage each other in living high standards." — For the Strength of Youth, 16

On his first night home from his mission, Jason (here and elsewhere, names of missionaries have been changed) was invited to the home of a friend where his old pre-mission buddies were anxious to get together with him. They were not members of the Church and really had no idea what Jason's missionary experience had been like or how he had changed. Most of the talk centered on girls, popular music, and the latest movies, things in which Jason had no interest at all. He realized that he had become a very different person over the past two years, but his friends had not changed that much. They had no comprehension of what he had experienced or how he had changed in the past two years. He went home early.

"I said my prayers, got into bed, and cried all night," he confessed. The next morning he went to the LDS Institute building near his home and found a new set of friends—a group of recently returned missionaries with whom he had more in common. He didn't forget about his old friends or ignore them, but he knew he needed strong friends who shared his values and understood his life.

Get Some New Clothes

This sounds simple, but it can be perplexing. Just remember that you don't need to completely change your wardrobe to match the latest style, and you don't need to buy everything all at once that you'll wear for the next two years. Take some time, and remember Elder L. Tom Perry's advice that you always want to look like a returned missionary.[1]

Get Busy

If your family wants to take a vacation together, great, but the busier you are the happier you will be. You are used to being fully occupied all day every day. Regardless of how long your gap is, stay busy and productive.

> "Get back to work as soon as possible. Ask for a calling, hopefully a teaching calling. It will help you to feel useful." — A returned missionary

If you don't have a job and school doesn't start for another two months, spend some time every day serving in the community and ward. You are accustomed to serving others all day long, and continuing to serve is essential to your continued happiness and progress. Get involved in family history, get in touch with your recent converts, go to the temple, go out with the

> *"Always stay busy doing something productive. Don't let yourself get lazy. Relax when needed, but do something exciting."*
> *— A returned elder*

missionaries, or ask your family or the bishop for the name of someone who needs some help. Stay productive and find ways to serve others.

Surfing the Internet, playing video games, watching television, or engaging in other unproductive activities will cause you to lose the spirit of your mission faster than almost anything else you could do. You may be exhausted from eighteen months or two years of constant hard work, but this is no time for a sabbatical. Get a good night's rest, recover from your jet lag, and get busy.

> *"Cease to be idle; cease to be unclean; cease to find fault one with another; cease to sleep longer than is needful; retire to thy bed early, that ye may not be weary; arise early, that your bodies and your minds may be invigorated." — Doctrine & Covenants 88:124*

Keep a Schedule

You don't need to keep the same schedule you kept in the mission field, but keep a schedule that begins each day with prayer and scripture study. Going to bed early, getting up early, praying, studying the scriptures, and exercising: these daily routines helped you be productive as a missionary, and they will help you maintain that productivity throughout your life.

🏃 Most returned missionaries find that getting up early every morning, even if you were up late the night before, is extremely valuable. The missionary schedule—up at 6:30 A.M. and in bed at 10:30 P.M.—is inspired, and it was a key to your productivity and success as a missionary. Making this a lifelong habit will reward you with many blessings.

Take Charge of Your Life

Before your mission, your parents may have taken care of many of your needs—food, shelter, clothing, and medical and dental care. While they may continue to provide many types of support and encouragement, you are now an adult and should take primary responsibility for your life. You probably haven't had a medical or dental checkup since your pre-mission checkup; take responsibility for scheduling medical and dental checkups. Begin taking responsibility for your housing and other necessities of life. This first week is a good time to talk with your parents and family about these issues.

> *"Doing the 'small and simple' things makes a big difference—wake up, pray, make your bed, shower. That routine makes the entire day go better."*
> *—A returned elder*

Read Your Patriarchal Blessing

You are moving into a wonderful and marvelous period of your life. Prayerfully read your patriarchal blessing to discern what the Lord has in store for you, and strive to understand and apply the inspired counsel it contains. As you study your patriarchal blessing regularly, you will continue to receive additional insight.

Patriarchal Blessings: Videos and Audio, http://www.lds.org/topics/patriarchal -blessings/video-audio

Don't "Adjust"

One of the questions you are likely to be asked over and over again during the first week and continuing for several months is, "Have you adjusted yet?" What many people really mean by this is, "Are you back to who you were yet?" The best answer is "No, nor do I intend to be who I once was." Well-meaning friends may be anxious to "break you in" when you return home. In fact, some of your greatest challenges will come from those closest to you — they recognize that you are different from who you were and they want you be "normal" — the person they remember. You have had amazing experiences, have seen miracles, have grown in ways even you can hardly comprehend. Why would you want to "adjust" or be "broken in?" You were probably a teenager when you left; the greatest tragedy of your mission would be to become a teenager again. You are not "normal" and hopefully never will be—you are extraordinary. Let others adjust to the new person you have become. Your mission changed you. You are, and will be for the rest of your life, a returned missionary. To paraphrase Winston Churchill, "Never, never, never adjust!"[2]

REMEMBER THIS

1. Your release is a new beginning, and the best of your life is ahead of you.

2. The gap between your release and starting school or work is especially important in your transition.

3. You have returned a very different person—don't revert to who you once were.

5

The Cornerstones of a Successful Transition

How firm a foundation . . .
Is laid for your faith.
Hymns, no. 85

Your mission was so rewarding and satisfying partly because it constantly forced you out of your comfort zone. You had experiences you had never had before because you did things you had never done before: you prayed more, studied the scriptures more, sought the direction of the Spirit more, and served others more. And as a result, you grew more and saw more miracles.

Not every aspect of missionary life can be transferred directly to your postmission life, but the valuable habits you developed as a missionary can continue to lift you and propel you forward just as they did on your mission. Note that none of the habits mentioned above — prayer, scripture study, being guided by the Spirit, and serving others — requires that you be called and set apart as a full-time missionary. The blessings that flow from those activities are available to all who do them.

ACTIVITY

Write the answers to the following questions in your study journal:

- Before your call as a full-time missionary, how many times a day did you pray? While you were a full-time missionary, how many times a day did you pray?

- Before your call as a full-time missionary, how much time did you spend each week studying the scriptures? While you were a full-time missionary, how much time did you spend each week studying the scriptures?

- Before your call as a full-time missionary, how often during the day did you consciously seek to be guided by the Holy Spirit? While you were a full-time missionary, how often during the day did you consciously seek to be guided by the Holy Spirit?

- Before your call as a full-time missionary, how much of your time and energy was spent focusing on and serving others? While you were a full-time missionary, how much of your time and energy was spent focusing on and serving others?

We asked a number of returned missionaries to rank the habits of successful returned missionaries. There was remarkable agreement about the four most important habits that help a returning missionary transition properly and continue to grow and progress in his or her life. As you move into this new and exciting phase of your life, here are four fundamental principles and habits—four cornerstones of life—that will result in continued growth, happiness, and success during the next two years and every year thereafter:

1. Pray regularly and frequently.
2. Study the scriptures every day.
3. Seek to be guided by the Spirit.
4. Attend the temple regularly and frequently.

Pray Regularly and Frequently

The scriptural injunction is to "always pray" (3 Nephi 18:19). Begin your day with prayer, pray throughout the day, and conclude your day with a report and an expression of gratitude in prayer. Make commitments to your Father in Heaven each morning, and account for your actions each night. Keep the prayer habits you developed as a missionary.

SCRIPTURE STUDY

Why is it important to pray always? What blessings flow from constant prayer? Record what you learn in your study journal.

Luke 21:36	Doctrine & Covenants 10:5
2 Nephi 32:9	Doctrine & Covenants 19:38
3 Nephi 18:15–21	Doctrine & Covenants 90:24

Study the Scriptures Every Day

As a missionary, you began each day with prayer followed by scripture study. Daily scripture study is one of the cornerstones upon which you build your life. Your missionary day included companion study as well as personal study, and having companion study after your mission is also valuable. Your companion may be your family, your roommates, or eventually your eternal companion. Your personal study is essential, but if you have the opportunity to study regularly with a companion, both you and your study companion will benefit.

> "A mission is preparation for life." – A returned sister

As a missionary, you focused most of your scripture study on finding teachings, insights and doctrine that would help your investigators. You will find that much of your scripture study now is to help you find answers to your questions, although you will continue to receive guidance as you study the scriptures and ponder the needs of others—family, friends, roommates, and colleagues.

The scriptures are the handbooks of life. In them you will find answers to questions about your own life and inspiration regarding how to help others. In them you will find peace, comfort, and direction.

> "Continue with your personal scripture study for an hour every day. Once you stop it is very difficult to pick up the habit again." – A returned sister

Elder Hugh W. Pinnock observed, "In a lifetime, each member can become a spiritual scriptorian."[1] Make daily scripture study a lifelong habit.

As a missionary, you kept a study journal to record what you learned and the inspiration you received while studying. As Elder Richard G. Scott taught, "Knowledge carefully recorded is knowledge available in time of need."[2] Recording what you learn and the inspiration you receive while studying is a habit that will benefit you throughout your life.

 "Companion Study" and "Study Journal," *Preach My Gospel,* https://www.lds.org /manual/preach-my-gospel-a-guide-to -missionary-service/introduction-how -can-i-best-use-preach-my-gospel

If you live near an institute of religion, consider enrolling in an institute class. Institute (or religion classes at a Church university) will give structure and support to your daily scripture study.

While you will want to study regularly all of the standard works, there is value in placing a particular emphasis on the Book of Mormon. President Gordon B. Hinckley said, "Without reservation I promise you that if you will prayerfully read the Book of Mormon, regardless of how many times you previously have read it, there will come into your hearts . . . the Spirit of the Lord. There will come a strengthened resolution to walk in obedience to his commandments, and there will come a stronger testimony of the living reality of the Son of God."[3] Consider making a personal commitment to read the entire Book of Mormon each year for the rest of your life. Some years you may wish to read it or listen to it in your mission language (if other than your native language). You learned as a missionary of the great converting power of the Book of Mormon. Reading it at least annually and reading from it daily will increase the depth and power of your own conversion.

Elder Jeffrey R. Holland, "Safety for the Soul," October 2009 general conference, http://www.lds.org/general-conference /2009/10/safety-for-the-soul

Seek to Be Guided by the Spirit

Preach My Gospel reminds us of this fundamental truth: "God loves you and all His children. He is anxious to support you in your practical and specific challenges. You have been promised inspiration to know what to do. . . . He will help you as you try to recognize and understand the Spirit through diligent scripture study."[4]

Many of the miracles you experienced as a missionary occurred as you sought throughout the day to feel and respond to the gentle promptings of the Spirit. President Brigham Young taught, "It is your privilege and duty to live so that you know when the word of

> *"Keep the gospel a part of your life, just as it was on your mission. Pray, study, serve, love. You should still strive to have the Spirit with you always, just like on the mission."*
> *— A returned elder*

the Lord is spoken to you and when the mind of the Lord is revealed to you."[5]

Strive at all times to be in a frame of mind and an environment where you can hear and feel the promptings of the Spirit. As you act on those promptings, you will continue to see miracles.

ACTIVITY

Preach My Gospel says, "Many voices in the world compete for your attention, and they can easily drown out spiritual impressions if you are not careful" (96). In your study journal, list some of the voices that compete for your attention and may make it difficult to hear and feel the promptings of the Spirit. What can you do to help quiet those voices so that you can hear the Spirit throughout the day?

Attend the Temple Regularly and Frequently

One mission president advised his returning missionaries that he would call them from time to time to ask a single question: When was the last time you went to the temple? The answer to that question would tell him everything he needed to know about how his former missionary was doing. As a missionary, you had very limited opportunities to attend the temple. But as a returned missionary, you should make the temple central to your life. Regular temple attendance provides you with the opportunity to serve others by acting as proxy for saving ordinances, reminds you of your own covenants, engages you in the work of salvation, and allows you to leave the outside world and find peace in the Lord's house.

If you live near a temple, you may want to volunteer to serve as a temple worker. You may be asked to work in the baptistry or in various other areas of the temple. Such service may require a commitment of only two to four hours each week.

> *"Going to the temple regularly was very helpful for me, especially since we didn't have one in our mission. It's easy to get distracted when you come home — especially by things that don't matter — so going to the temple helps you keep an eternal perspective."*
> *— A returned sister*

ACTIVITY

Set goals and make plans: When and where will you have personal and family prayers? When and where will you study the scriptures daily? What will you do to seek and follow the promptings of the Spirit? When and how often will you attend the temple? Create a simple schedule for the next few weeks that will help you accomplish those goals. Record your schedule in your study journal or planner.

Elder L. Tom Perry, "The Returned Missionary," October 2001 general conference, http://www.lds.org/general-conference/2001/10/the-returned-missionary

REMEMBER THIS

1. Pray regularly and frequently.

2. Study the scriptures every day.

3. Seek to be guided by the Spirit.

4. Attend the temple regularly and frequently.

6
Other Elements of a Strong Foundation

Let us then press boldly onward.
Hymns, no. 276

The four principles of praying, studying the scriptures, seeking the guidance of the Spirit, and attending the temple are the cornerstones of a successful transition from great missionary to great returned missionary. They provide points of anchor upon which the rest of your life will be built.

But a strong foundation requires more than just cornerstones; the cornerstones must be connected with strong foundation walls. In interviews and discussions with many returned missionaries, we learned several other important habits that contribute to a successful transition from missionary life.

Attend All Your Church Meetings

Sundays were usually intense for you as a missionary. You were busy helping investigators get to Church meetings, shepherding them while they were there, and following up afterwards. For at least the first few Sundays after you return home, you may have no obligation except to attend your meetings. Be an active worshipper and an active participant in classes—raise your hand, share experiences, ask inspired questions. Go out of your way to meet people you don't know and learn their names. Several returned missionaries gave this very simple counsel: "Attend all three hours of Church meetings every Sunday."

You may want to attend your family ward for the first few Sundays you are home, but you may also have the option of attending a Young Single Adult ward. Whatever you decide, get involved with your chosen ward and attend the entire block of meetings every Sunday.

Always Have a Church Calling

You are accustomed to being fully engaged in building the kingdom, and receiving and magnifying a calling is an important part of your postmission life. Bishops have a lot on their plate, and they may not focus on getting you a calling for several weeks. It's okay to be persistent. Don't hesitate to tell the bishop you would like a calling *now*. If you live near a temple, you could express your interest in being a veil worker or temple worker (that makes it easy for the bishop, as he does not have to work you into the ward organization). Always have a calling, and strive to fulfill and magnify it.

Find Opportunities to Serve Others

One of the most satisfying aspects of being a full-time missionary is that your own needs were minimal and largely taken care of by others: you could focus all your energy on trying to help others, including your investigators, the members, and your companion. One of your challenges when you return from your mission is that you will have to spend some time and energy on your own education, financial security, social life, etc. — as one returned missionary put it, "You have permission to think of yourself."

But your greatest joy will still come from serving others. Find opportunities every day to serve someone else — your family, your roommates, your friends, even strangers. Get involved in your Church calling. Donate time at the local food kitchen, the homeless shelter, or Bishop's Storehouse. One returned missionary, after three years at home, wrote, "Give service at every opportunity! The goodness you felt while serving on your mission doesn't magically disappear when you are home. It can be found in raking your neighbors' leaves or shoveling snow from their driveway."

> *"The greatest postmission joy has come from asking myself two questions: Who can I help? How can I help them? And then acting on impressions that come."* — A returned sister

If you are feeling a little lost, remember that the best way to find yourself is to lose yourself in the service of others.

Set Goals and Make Plans

Goal setting and planning are some of the most important and useful skills you learned as a missionary. You had weekly planning sessions and daily planning sessions, and you often revised plans throughout the day. Chapter 8 of this book will help you adapt your mission goal setting and planning skills to postmission life.

Keep Busy and Productive

If you are in school, study hard. Get a job and even a second job if you need to. Don't hesitate to push yourself. As one missionary said, "Stay focused and move fast." Remember how hard you worked as a missionary and how satisfying it was to work hard. Don't be afraid to lengthen your stride, quicken your pace, and stretch yourself. Focusing on productive, meaningful actions will help you achieve your goals. The more you attempt to do, the greater your capacity will become. You don't need to run faster than you are able, but you can probably run faster than you think you can. Don't shortchange yourself.

Date

As awkward as you may feel, developing healthy friendships with members of the opposite sex is now an important part of your life. More on this in chapter 10.

Continue to Engage in Missionary Work

Few activities in life bring the same satisfaction as inviting others to come unto Christ by helping them develop faith in Jesus Christ, repent, receive priesthood ordinances, enjoy the gift the of Holy Ghost, and endure to the end. With recent changes in Church curriculum and policy, there is a new urgency about missionary work. More on this in chapter 11.

Keep a Journal

Many blessings flow from keeping a journal. One of the most valuable is that it helps you see the daily miracles in your life. Strive to have an experience every day that is journal worthy—an experience, however simple and small it may be, that makes you aware that God loves you and that He can use you to serve His children.

 Brad Wilcox, "Why Write It?" *Ensign,* Sept. 1999, http://www.lds.org/ensign/1999/09 /why-write-it

ACTIVITY

Talk to or write to three or four well-grounded returned missionaries who have been home longer than you. Ask them to describe the most useful lessons they learned about the transition home. Ask them what advice they have for you as a newly returned missionary. Record their responses in your study journal.

REMEMBER THIS

1. Attend all your Church meetings.

2. Always have a Church calling.

3. Find opportunities to serve others.

4. Set goals and make plans.

5. Keep busy and productive.

6. Date.

7. Continue to engage in missionary work.

8. Keep a journal.

7

How to Write Your Own Handbook

In this there is safety; in this there is peace.
Hymns, no. 303

As hard as it was, your life as a missionary was very easy in many ways. You did not need to worry about your schedule (it was defined in the *Missionary Handbook* and *Preach My Gospel*); you did not need to worry about money (it appeared almost magically each month on your debit card); your housing was provided for you (primitive as it may have been); you did not have to worry about dating (it was prohibited); you didn't even have to find your own roommate (companions were assigned by the mission president). You only had to focus on one thing: your missionary purpose. The *Missionary Handbook* and *Preach My Gospel* answered nearly every question you had and addressed nearly every concern.

Now overnight your life has become much more complex: you need to think about your education, your future career, a job, a place to live, roommates, paying bills, and finding an eternal companion. And you no longer have a handbook. That's why it can be very helpful to write your own postmission handbook.

Your Daily Schedule

A good place to start is with your daily schedule. While you were a missionary, your schedule was the same every day, with some minor modifications on Sunday, preparation day, and weekly planning day. And it never really changed throughout your mission. When you left the mission home to travel to your own home, that consistent schedule disappeared, but that does not mean you should not have a schedule. Having a schedule is essential to a successful transition and to your continued growth and progress.

> *"Making a schedule right when you get home is key. . . . It can be as simple as just setting up things in the day — studies, working out, helping around the house, hanging out with your friends, going on dates." — A returned elder*

As you develop your schedule, start by scheduling the next seven days, then use that model to create a longer-term schedule. Your schedule might be different on different days because of your job, class schedule, family obligations, and Church calling. But try to establish regular times for such daily activities as prayer, scripture study, physical exercise, and planning.

As you create your schedule, consider the following:

- While you were a missionary, your day always began with a morning devotional—personal and companion prayer, personal and companion scripture study. This is a valuable pattern to continue after your mission, as it will help you feel to the promptings of the Spirit throughout the day.

- Consider your work schedule, your class schedule, and your Church calling, and include those commitments in your schedule.

> "A piece of advice that helped me came about two years after I had come home from my mission. In a conversation with my mission president, he taught me that I could 'prayerfully rewrite the white handbook at each stage of life.' While this may be obvious to some, I needed to realize that I was now in a different phase of life and I could live by different rules."
> — A returned sister

- Include times for regular exercise. This could be part of your morning routine (as it was in the mission field), or it might work better at a different time of day.

- Include times for planning—daily, weekly, and monthly.

- Consider the need for family and social time, personal reading, and recreation.

As your obligations and priorities change, your schedule also will need to change. For instance, if you are in school, you will need to create a new schedule each term as your class schedule changes. If your work schedule changes, make the appropriate changes in your weekly schedule.

Once you start working, going to school, or both, your scheduling becomes quite simple as most of your day will be filled with previously scheduled activities. You may find that you need to pay particular attention to scheduling time for study and appropriate social and recreational activities.

Many people today keep their schedule on an electronic device, such as a computer or smart phone. This works well because you can access your schedule from almost anywhere (just as you could access anytime the daily planner you carried with you during your mission). You may find it useful, however, to create your schedule on paper first and then enter the scheduled events into your electronic calendar. Find a method that works for you.

ACTIVITY

Review the missionary schedule found in the *Missionary Handbook,* 14–15, and *Preach My Gospel,* viii. Then create your own daily and weekly schedule and record them in your study journal.

Principles and Standards

The *Missionary Handbook* contains "principles and standards" that are designed to "protect you physically and spiritually."[1] Standards are specific rules—the mission rules. There are specific rules for most of the situations you encountered as a missionary, but because a pocket-size handbook cannot have a rule for every situation, the *Missionary Handbook* also contains principles to guide you in the absence of a specific rule. For example, the *Handbook* contains very specific rules regarding dress and grooming ("Always wear a white shirt with a tie that is conservative in color, pattern, width, and length"), but it also includes this principle: "Never allow your appearance or your behavior to draw attention away from your message or your calling."[2]

Now that you are a returned missionary, not all of the old mission rules apply. You are no longer required to wear a white shirt and a conservative tie every day or to always stay with your companion. As a missionary, you avoided television, movies, popular music, magazines, newspapers, and most Internet sites. As a returned missionary, you no longer have the mission rules to protect you, but you can establish your own principles and standards that will protect you both physically and spiritually.

Elder Hartman J. Rector Jr., formerly a United States Navy pilot and member of the Seventy, taught the following in general conference:

"In my experience, I have found that it is very, very dangerous to fly just high enough to miss the treetops. I spent twenty-six years flying the navy's airplanes. It was very exciting to see how close I could fly to the trees. This is called 'flat hatting' in the navy, and it is extremely dangerous. When you are flying just high enough to miss the trees and your engine coughs once, you are in the trees.

"Now let's pretend that the navy had a commandment—'Thou shalt not fly thy airplane in the trees.' As a matter of fact, they did have such a commandment. In order to really be free of the commandment, it becomes necessary for me to add a commandment of my own to the navy's commandment, such as, 'Thou shalt not fly thy airplane closer than 5,000 feet to the trees.' When you do this, you make the navy's commandment of not flying in the trees easy to live, and the safety factor is tremendously increased."[3]

The commandments are your guide; they are the rules we have covenanted to live by. But as you write your own handbook, you may want to create some personal rules that keep you well within the margin of safety. Some examples based on Elder Rector's example include the following:

- Never go into a house alone with a person of the opposite sex.
- Never, never go into a bedroom alone with a person of the opposite sex.
- Do not watch R- or X-rated movies.
- Do not spend time in drinking or gambling establishments.

Elder Hartman J. Rector Jr., "Live above the Law to Be Free," October 1972 general conference, http://www.lds.org/general-conference/1972/10/live-above-the-law-to-be-free

Creating Your Own Principles and Standards

One of the best resources you have as you write your own standards is *For the Strength of Youth*. Because it is written primarily for youth, *For the Strength of Youth* sometimes is overlooked by adults, but the inspired principles and standards it contains can be easily adapted to every phase of life. Consider using it as you craft your personal handbook. Here are some thoughts about principles and standards you might want to include.

For the Strength of Youth, https://www.lds.org/bc/content/shared/content/english/pdf/ForTheStrengthOfYouth-eng.pdf

Dress and appearance. As a missionary, you were asked to dress and groom the same way that Church leaders — General Authorities and general presidencies of the auxiliaries (the Relief Society, Young Women, and Primary) — dress and groom. While you are no longer required to wear a white shirt and conservative tie or a nice dress or Sunday skirt every day, as a returned missionary you should always "look the part."[4] We know of one stake presidency that invites the returned elders in their stake to keep their hair short and well combed and to avoid facial hair.

Consider making a commitment to always dress like a leader — white shirt, appropriate tie, and jacket for men, and appropriate Sunday dress for women — at Church meetings. Dressing your best at church is a simple way to show your love and respect for the Savior as you participate in sacred ordinances.

Elder Jeffrey R. Holland counseled that "wherever possible a white shirt be worn by the deacons, teachers, and priests who handle the sacrament. For sacred ordinances in the Church we often use ceremonial clothing, and a white shirt could be seen as a gentle reminder of the white clothing you wore in the baptismal font and an anticipation of the white shirt you will soon wear into the temple and onto your missions.

> "Your dress and grooming influence the way you and others act. . . . Avoid being extreme or inappropriately casual in clothing, hairstyle, and behavior. . . . Show respect for the Lord and yourself by dressing appropriately for Church meetings and activities. . . . Ask yourself, 'Would I feel comfortable with my appearance if I were in the Lord's presence?'" — For the Strength of Youth, 6–8

"That simple suggestion is not intended to be pharisaic

or formalistic. We do not want deacons or priests in uniforms or unduly concerned about anything but the purity of their lives. But how our young people dress can teach a holy principle to us all, and it certainly can convey sanctity. As President David O. McKay taught, a white shirt contributes to the sacredness of the holy sacrament (see Conference Report, Oct. 1956, p. 89)."[5]

How you dress and groom yourself affects the service you are able to render. You never want to limit your availability to officiate in priesthood ordinances or to serve in other ways. For example, there is no commandment regarding facial hair for men, but current policy requires male temple ordinance workers to be clean-shaven. While dress and grooming cannot qualify you for service, they may preclude you from certain types of service.

ACTIVITY

Review "Dress and Appearance," *For the Strength of Youth,* 6–8. Prayerfully consider your personal standards for dress and appearance, and write them in your study journal.

Entertainment and media. Few things can rob you of the Spirit faster than inappropriate entertainment and media. *For the Strength of Youth* gives this very clear and simple standard: "Do not attend, view, or participate in anything that is vulgar, immoral, violent, or pornographic in any way."[6] One returned missionary created a personal rule to refrain from watching any television. His comment: "I haven't missed anything worthwhile!"

You enjoyed the companionship of the Spirit on your mission in large measure because you avoided most media and listened only to music that invited the Spirit. Inappropriate movies, videos, television, video games, music, books, magazines, or inappropriate websites will dull your spiritual sensitivity. "Avoid pornography at all costs."[7] Never click out of curiosity, never linger on an inappropriate image.

Numerous studies have demonstrated that playing violent video games significantly increases aggressive behavior and numbs the player to the pain and suffering of others.[8]

The good news is, once you have made the decision to avoid such media and set appropriate personal standards to safeguard yourself, the Spirit will protect you and give you clear guidance on what to avoid. You have complete control over what you see, read, watch, listen to, and do. Choosing wisely will bless your life.

ACTIVITY

Review "Entertainment and Media," and "Music and Dancing," *For the Strength of Youth,* 11–13 and 22–23. Prayerfully establish personal standards for entertainment and media, and write them in your study journal.

Language. Not only does your language communicate to others who you are but the words you use and how you communicate shape how you feel and who you are. Learn to read, write, and speak well. Build a good vocabulary. Learn how to express humor without belittling others. As in other aspects of your life, the General Authorities and general auxiliary presidencies are good models. Take advantage of every opportunity to see them, hear them, and read their writings. Then try to emulate them.

When you wore a missionary name tag, you always used refined and dignified language when speaking, writing, texting, etc. As a returned missionary who covenants weekly to take the Savior's name upon you, make sure your language always reflects who you are. Eliminate from your vocabulary words and phrases that would not be used by prophets and apostles.

> *"Language is one of your most powerful tools. Be conscious of how you speak, and strive for humility, dignity, and simplicity in your language. Refined, dignified language will clearly identify you as a servant of the Lord."* — Missionary Handbook, 8

ACTIVITY

Review the *Missionary Handbook,* 8–9, and "Language," *For the Strength of Youth,* 20–21. Prayerfully consider your personal standards for language, and write them in your study journal.

Physical and emotional health. "The Word of Wisdom," said President Boyd K. Packer, "does not promise you perfect health, but it teaches how to keep the body you were born with in the best condition and your mind alert to delicate spiritual promptings."[9] Strive to be physically and emotionally healthy. Your body is a sacred vessel for your spirit and is a gift from the Lord. Living the Word of Wisdom and keeping your body healthy enables you to be more sensitive to the promptings of the Spirit.

Develop good habits of nutrition and exercise, strive to maintain a healthy weight and avoid excessive use of soft drinks, caffeine-laden "energy" drinks, and sugar-laden foods with little nutritional value. A key to good health is developing the discipline required to care for your body. Eat well, get adequate sleep and exercise, get regular medical and dental checkups, and keep your immunizations current.

G. Craig Kiser, "A Principle with Promises," *Ensign*, Feb. 2014, https://www.lds.org /ensign/2014/02/a-principle-with-promises

You are the best observer of your own physical and mental health. No one is free from sickness and disease in this mortal life. Know where to find a doctor and dentist. Get help when you need it.

Mental and emotional illness is real, and it is not uncommon among young people. If you have concerns, discuss them with your parents, a priesthood leader, or a licensed counselor. Don't hesitate to get professional help if you feel you need it.

Elder Jeffrey R. Holland, "Like a Broken Vessel," October 2013 general conference, http://www.lds.org/general-conference/2013/10/like-a-broken-vessel

ACTIVITY

Review "Physical and Emotional Health," *For the Strength of Youth*, 25–27. Prayerfully establish your personal standards regarding physical and emotional health. Write them in your study journal.

Keep the Sabbath day holy. As a missionary, you taught others about the blessings of keeping the Sabbath day holy. You extended invitations and promised blessings regarding this important commandment. Now that you are faced with more choices regarding how you spend your time on the Sabbath, remember the invitations you made and the blessings you promised. As a returned missionary, you will find that most of your days are consumed with school, work, and other important

"When you are a missionary, every day feels like Sunday. After a mission, Sundays become a special day to recharge and refocus on the Savior. Sundays became a day to cherish. I now look forward to Sundays as a very special day to become clean and take my questions to the Lord." – A returned sister

concerns. Sunday provides an important rest from your daily labors and an opportunity to recharge your spirit and renew your covenants. Consider what things you will do on Sundays, what things you will not do, and how you will dress so that the entire day remains a holy day, set apart from the other days of the week.

> **ACTIVITY**
>
> Review *Preach My Gospel,* 74, and "Sabbath Day Observance," *For the Strength of Youth,* 30–31. Talk to someone you respect about his or her personal guidelines for keeping the Sabbath day holy. Prayerfully establish your own personal standards for keeping the Sabbath day holy, and write them in your study journal.

Personal finances. Financial management as a missionary was simple—all you had to do was make sure your monthly allotment lasted all month. Now that you're home, learning how to properly manage your personal finances is essential to your future success and happiness. Here are some simple guidelines:

1. Pay the Lord first. Always pay an honest tithe, and be generous in your other offerings.

2. Spend less than you earn. Establish a simple budget and live by it. You can never earn enough money to compensate for poor management of your finances.

Emergencies always come—build up some financial reserve.

3. Learn and practice self-discipline and restraint. Manage your expectations. When you are in your twenties, you can't afford to have all the things that your parents had when they were in their fifties.

4. Avoid debt like the plague. Elder Marvin J. Ashton of the Council of the Twelve Apostles counseled that debt be used only for the purchase of a home and obtaining an education, and even then, debt should be kept at a minimum.[10]

> *"With the exception of buying a* home, *paying for* education, *or making* other vital investments, *avoid debt and the resulting finance charges. Buy consumer durables and vacations with cash. Avoid installment credit, and be careful with your use of credit cards. . . . Buy used items until you have saved sufficiently to purchase quality new items."*
> — *Elder Marvin J. Ashton,* One for the Money, 6; *emphasis added*

One for the Money: Guide to Family Finances, http://www.lds.org/bc/content /shared/content/english/pdf/language -materials/33293_eng.pdf

---

ACTIVITY

Review "Keep the Law of Tithing," *Preach My Gospel,* 78–79; "Sexual Purity," *For the Strength of Youth,* 35–37; and *One for the Money.* Prayerfully establish personal standards for wise financial management, and write them in your study journal.

Virtue and purity. Purity is power, and it is essential to happiness. As a missionary, you taught the Lord's fundamental standard regarding sexual purity: "Do not have any sexual relations before marriage, and be completely faithful to your spouse after marriage."[11] But you will need to set your own boundaries that will help you maintain virtue and avoid the evil influences of the world, influences that will dull your spiritual sensitivity and deny you the blessings that flow from fully keeping the covenants you have made and hope to make.

> *"Pre-mission addictions are not more powerful than the agency God has given you. Blessings of the Atonement will continue to heal and sanctify you just as they applied to your investigators." — A former mission president*

As you begin dating, set clear guidelines. You are dating with the goal of marriage, and your dating guidelines may be different from what they were before your mission. But you are not married: don't do things that only married people should do. *For the Strength of Youth* gives clear standards: "Before marriage, do not participate in passionate kissing, lie on top of another person, or touch the private, sacred parts of another person's body, with or without clothing."[12]

Great strength and joy come from staying pure. *For the Strength of Youth* counsels: "Do not do anything else that arouses [sexual] emotions in your own body. . . . Do not participate in discussions or any media that arouse sexual feelings. Do not participate in any kind of pornography."[13]

Set clear boundaries for yourself, commit to always stay within those boundaries, and pay attention to the spiritual promptings that will help you remain clean and virtuous. Your goal is to be sealed in the temple, and the key to temple worthiness is to keep the covenants that you have already made in the temple.

ACTIVITY

Review *Preach My Gospel,* page 77, and *For the Strength of Youth,* pages 35–37. Prayerfully establish appropriate personal standards that will help you remain virtuous and pure. Write them in your study journal.

Social media. Social media can be a wonderful thing. Most mission presidents maintain social media groups for their missionaries, and it is a great way to keep in touch with your mission president, former companions, members, converts, and former investigators. It can be used effectively to continue to share the gospel message with others. You can use social media to "sweep the earth with messages filled with righteousness and truth—messages that are authentic, edifying, and praiseworthy."[14]

Elder David A. Bednar, "To Sweep the Earth as with a Flood," https://www.lds.org/prophets-and-apostles/unto-all-the-world/to-sweep-the-earth-as-with-a-flood

Social media, however, can be a two-edged sword. You may want to set personal standards limiting the amount of time you spend on social media and the Internet, as well as standards for how you will use these powerful tools.

Your "virtual persona" as seen by others on social media sites should reflect who you are and who you are striving to become: a true disciple of Christ. Never use words, language, or images that in any way might be considered inappropriate. Be very careful to avoid sharing links or posts that may contain inappropriate language or photographs. You may take photographs of yourself at the pool or the beach, but do you really want photographs of you partially clothed posted on the Internet for all the world to see? Before posting a comment, a photograph, or a link, ask yourself if the prophet would post that comment, photograph, or link. Would you be comfortable with him seeing

> *"There are people I never see except on social media. When they put something up that may be questionable, I can't help but think differently about them."*
> *— A returned elder*

your post? Would you want a prospective employer to see your post? (Many employers review social media sites before making a job offer.) Would you want your converts to see your post? How might your post influence them? Before clicking Post, ask yourself, "Is this post 'honest, true, chaste, benevolent [kind], virtuous?'" (Articles of Faith 1:13).

 "Five Questions to Ask Before You Click 'Post,'" http://brillanrayos.blogspot.com /2014/02/five-questions-to-ask-before -you-click.html

ACTIVITY

Review what you have read and learned about dress and appearance, language, entertainment and media, and virtue and purity. Prayerfully establish appropriate personal standards regarding use of social media, and write them in your study journal.

There are many other standards you may want to include in your personal handbook. The scriptures are your primary resource. *For the Strength of Youth*, recent general conference addresses, and articles in the *Ensign* and on lds.org are all important and useful additions to the scriptures. As you study each morning, you may wish to review, revise, and add to your personal handbook based on the promptings you receive.

REMEMBER THIS

1. Establishing and following an appropriate daily and weekly schedule will help you be productive and happy.

2. Establishing and following appropriate personal standards will protect you from the forces of the adversary.

8

"Set Goals and Make Plans"

Let God and heaven be your goal.
Hymns, no. 239

Set goals and make plans." That phrase appears a dozen times in *Preach My Gospel,* and for good reason. Although hard work is essential to success, many people work hard but never achieve very much because their efforts are unfocused. Like undisciplined swimmers, they expend a lot of energy paddling around and staying afloat but never cover very much distance. They keep their heads above water but never get anywhere. Working hard is essential to your success, but working hard is not enough: goals will focus your efforts so that your hard work will propel you forward.

> *"Someone has said the trouble with not having a goal is that you can spend your life running up and down the field and never crossing the goal line."*
> — *President Thomas S. Monson,* Teachings of Thomas S. Monson, *123*

While still in high school, Rodney H. Brady devoted many hours to setting goals and determining what he needed to do to achieve those goals. He created a list of two hundred goals, including serving a mission, getting a good education, serving in a high government position, running a large corporation, and being a university president. By age sixty-five he had, among other things, served as a missionary in

> *"Goals reflect the desires of our hearts and our vision of what we can accomplish."* — Preach My Gospel, 145

Great Britain; obtained a doctorate from Harvard; served as assistant secretary for administration and management in the U.S. Department of Health, Education, and Welfare; served as president and CEO of Bonneville International; and served as president of Weber State University.

His advice? "A goal-oriented life is far more likely to lead to success than is a life that leaves success to chance."[1]

In fact, President Thomas S. Monson has taught, "Without a goal there can be no real success."[2]

As a missionary, you set monthly, weekly, and daily goals. You spent several hours each week setting goals and making plans to achieve those goals. And you became accustomed to frequently asking yourself, "Does this activity help me achieve my goals?" Continuing to devote time and energy to setting goals and making plans is essential to achieving success in life.

Refine Your Goals

In chapter 3, you created a list of goals. You may want to prayerfully review and revise that list as you study this chapter. Here are some guidelines that others have found useful when setting goals.

- **A goal not written is only a wish.** Whatever the reason is, the act of writing down our goals greatly increases the likelihood that we will achieve our goals.
  It isn't enough to just have an idea of what your goals are. You are unlikely to achieve them if you can't articulate them clearly and put them in writing.

- **"Be specific and realistic, but set goals that will make you stretch."**[3] The more specific your goal is, the better you are able to make plans to achieve it. Goals should be achievable—setting a goal that is impossible to reach can create discouragement—but goals should be ambitious. Don't settle for mediocrity.

> *"Goals not written down are seldom measured, almost always lack structure, usually go unprioritized, are not systematically reviewed and updated, and are easily forgotten."*
> — *Rodney H. Brady,*
> Goal-Oriented Life, 8

- **Goals should be worthwhile.** Doing things right is important, but doing the right things right is much more important. Set meaningful goals that will make a difference in your life and who you become.

- **Share your goals.** Some goals may be personal and shared only with your Father in Heaven, but most goals are better shared with others. Sharing goals with others creates additional accountability. When you share your goals with others, you establish a support group that can provide encouragement and help.

- **Be flexible**. Your goals may change from time to time. Age, maturity, education level, health, family circumstances, and resources all change, and your goals should be flexible enough to accommodate these changes. If a goal is no longer relevant, cross it off your list. If a goal needs to be revised, revise it.

You may want to set goals in many areas of your life—spiritual development, education, marriage and family, career, personal finances, and personal health and fitness. Grouping related goals together can help you establish effective plans to achieve your goals.

Education should be a major focus for most recently returned missionaries, and educational goals should be included in your goal setting. Chapter 9 provides additional guidance on getting an education.

Sometimes setting spiritual goals may seem difficult— how do you measure spiritual progress? It is generally easier to set goals for things we want to *do* than for who we want to *be*. The Attribute Activity on page 126 of *Preach My Gospel* provides a template for how to set goals and make plans to become a disciple of Christ. Using this as a guide to set goals and measure progress can help you develop Christlike qualities and become the person you want to become.

Planning Is More Than Calendaring

Setting goals, of course, is only the first step. To achieve your goals, you must make and carry out specific plans. Devoting sufficient time and energy to planning will make your life productive now, just as it did during your mission. Remember that planning is different from calendaring or scheduling. Plans are *what* you want to do; calendaring is *when* you will do them. If all you do is calendar, in effect you turn control of your life over to others—school, work, and friends. Planning puts you in control of your life and is essential to achieving your goals.

> *"Keep planning! Planning helps me to keep my day nicely scheduled so I do not waste time doing pointless activities (such as Facebook). It helps keep me busy, and it helps me keep my priorities straight."*
> — *A returned elder*

Weekly Planning

Review your goals each week at a specific time—Sunday evening is often a good time for weekly planning. Plan *what* you will do, and schedule *when* you will do it. As a missionary, you followed very specific steps during your weekly planning session. Now that you are a returned missionary, your planning is probably simpler, but the basics are the same:

1. Pray for and seek inspiration.
2. Review your goals and plans for the previous week, recording your progress and your achievements.
3. Review your list of goals, including your long-term goals, and establish appropriate weekly goals. Write down *what* you will do and *when* you will do it.

Monthly Planning

In addition to a weekly planning session, you can benefit from a monthly planning session in which you set goals and make plans for the entire month. You might want to use your first weekly planning session each month to review last month's goals and then review goals and make plans for the new month.

Annual Planning

Many people are accustomed to making New Year's resolutions. Having an annual planning session is a very valuable practice. This is a good time to review your significant goals in life, assess your progress, make adjustments, and establish plans that will carry you forward towards your goals. Consider taking a day or two for an annual planning retreat—a time when you can get away from your daily activities and focus on where you have been, where you are, where you are going, and where you want to be. Such a planning retreat helps keep married couples working together on mutual goals and strengthening their relationship.

When we had several young children, we would do this two or three times a year, sometimes for just a few hours. It was one of the best things we did during the very busy years of raising a young family.

Daily Planning

Finally, don't neglect daily planning. As a missionary, you devoted time each day to planning. If you are a student or working full-time (or both), you can probably plan each day in a few minutes. But it is extremely valuable to take a minute or two each morning to review your weekly and daily plan so that you are aware of your goals throughout the day. Then when something comes up that is not in your schedule (and this happens regularly), you can make an intelligent decision and determine if or how you should change your plan for the day.

ACTIVITY

Prayerfully review and revise the list of goals you made in chapter 3. Write each major goal at the top of a page, and then write down what you need to do to achieve that goal.

You could do this in your study journal, in a separate notebook, or in an electronic document. You may need several weeks to complete this activity.

President Thomas S. Monson counseled, "Perfection is not achieved simply by wishing or hoping for it to come. It is approached as we establish specific goals in our lives and strive for their successful accomplishment."[4] Set goals, make plans, and work hard. This formula will almost certainly guarantee success. And the failure to set goals and make plans will almost certainly guarantee aimless drifting.

REMEMBER THIS

1. Hard work, though essential to success, is not enough. Setting goals and making plans will focus your efforts and enable you to achieve lasting success.

2. The planning skills you learned as a missionary will help you achieve success in life.

3. Having regular planning sessions will help you achieve your goals.

9

The Importance of Education

There is no end to wisdom. . . .
There is no end to truth.
Hymns, no. 284

For most recently returned missionaries, education is a primary focus. President Gordon B. Hinckley frequently counseled, "Get all the education you can."[1] Whether your interest is in advanced academics, technology, or skilled labor, education is essential to your success. President Joseph Fielding Smith said simply, "We believe in education."[2]

President Thomas S. Monson counseled, "This is your day of preparation, that you might meet the days of decision which are before you."[3]

Now is the time to focus on your education. Make it a top priority, work hard, study hard, and be a serious student. "Be willing to work diligently and make sacrifices if necessary."[4]

It would be hard to overemphasize the importance of education. Your "education will prepare you for greater service in the world and in the Church."[5] Getting a good

"Education," https://www.lds.org/topics
/education

education now will enable you to better support your-self and your family, raise your children, and serve in the Church. The Lord has invested heavily in you as a mission-ary; He expects you to continue to educate your mind and your hands in order to make a contribution to the world and His work.

President Brigham Young's advice is characteristically direct: "Go to school and study. . . . Put forth your ability to learn as fast as you can."[6] President Gordon B. Hinckley added, "Sacrifice for it, work for it, save for it, plan for it, and do it."[7] You—and your spouse, children, and grandchil-dren—will be blessed by your commitment to learning.

You may not yet have chosen a field of study nor de-cided upon a career. Talking with successful adults in ca-reers in which you have an interest can help you decide, as can taking a few classes in different areas of interest. If you are in college, consider taking classes from the best instruc-tors, regardless of the subject. The old adage, "Take profes-sors, not classes," has some truth to it: you may find these professors have a greater long-term effect on your life than those classes required for your graduation.

To decide upon a field of study, as in other important

decisions, the Lord requires that "you must study it out in your mind; then you must ask me if it be right" (D&C 9:8). Be prayerful, do your part, and keep moving forward. The Lord will open up the way as you act with diligence and faith.

> "For members of the Church, education is not merely a good idea — it's a commandment."
> — President Dieter F. Uchtdorf, "Two Principles for Any Economy," 58

Study with the objective of establishing yourself in a career that will enable you to support a family. This counsel applies equally to men and to women. Many sisters may find themselves in a position where they have to support themselves and even their families. Having a degree and skills that qualify one for good employment is always advantageous.

Lifelong Learning

As you establish educational goals, remember that education is more than just training for a job. President Thomas S. Monson stated, "Education is a process, not a completed act."[8] Learn how to learn, develop the habit of learning, and continue to learn all your life.

Read (a Lot)

One of the most important habits you can develop is to read. Reading is the key to continuing education. Read "out of the best books" (D&C 88:118) — the scriptures, history, biography, the sciences, good literature, the classics. President Brigham Young taught, "I would advise you to read books

> *"Very few among us read too much; most of us read too little." – President Joseph Fielding Smith,* Joseph Fielding Smith *[manual], 145*

that are worth reading; read reliable history, and search wisdom out of the best books you can procure."[9] Choose great books to read, and don't squander time by reading too much popular fiction and fantasy. Put down the smart phone, the tablet, and the laptop, turn off the television and the video game, and read out of the best books.

Broaden Your Knowledge

Doctrine and Covenants 88:78–79 states, "Teach ye diligently and my grace shall attend you, that you may be instructed more perfectly in theory, in principle, in doctrine, in the law of the gospel, in all things that pertain unto the kingdom of God, that are expedient for you to understand; of things both in heaven and in the earth, and under the earth; things which have been, things which are, things which must shortly come to pass; things which are at home, things which are abroad; the wars and the perplexities of the nations, and the judgments which are on the land; and a knowledge also of countries and of kingdoms."

The prophets have encouraged us to study every useful branch of knowledge. President Brigham Young said, "There is nothing I would like better than to learn chemistry, botany, geology, and mineralogy, so that I could tell what I walk on, the properties of the air I breathe, what I drink, etc."[10] President Dieter F. Uchtdorf reminded us that the best books can become a university, a classroom where we can always be learning: "Strive to increase your knowledge of all that is 'virtuous, lovely, or of good report or praiseworthy.'"[11]

Study Eternal Truths

President Joseph Fielding Smith taught that "the most important knowledge in the world is gospel knowledge. . . . It is far more important to know that Jesus Christ is our Redeemer, that he has given unto us the principles of eternal life, than it is to know all that can be obtained in secular education."[12] Some fields of learning are more valuable than others. The most useful branch of knowledge is that which concerns the eternal truths contained in the gospel of Jesus Christ.

> *"You cannot keep the commandments of the Lord and walk in righteousness unless you know what they are." – President Joseph Fielding Smith,* Joseph Fielding Smith *[manual], 144*

"Let us learn of Christ," counseled President Uchtdorf. "Let us seek out that knowledge which leads to peace, truth, and the sublime mysteries of eternity."[13] Elder Bruce R. McConkie observed that "we can consecrate a portion of our time to systematic study, to becoming gospel scholars, to treasuring up the revealed truths which guide us in paths of truth and righteousness."[14] A lifelong habit of daily, prayerful scripture study can help us become gospel scholars.

REMEMBER THIS

1. Education is a top priority in your life right now. Work hard and be diligent to obtain an education that prepares you for a successful career.

2. Develop a habit of lifelong learning.

3. Read a lot.

4. Broaden your knowledge.

5. Strive to become a gospel scholar.

10

Dating and Marriage

More purity give me, . . .
More, Savior, like thee.
Hymns, no. 131

The most important thing you will ever do in your life is to marry the right person at the right time in the right place. Now that you are a returned missionary, your social life has a renewed importance and higher purpose.

The Right Place

The right place to marry is in the temple. As a missionary, you worked hard to help others obtain the blessings of a temple sealing. Now do this for yourself. One of the most important things you can do to prepare for a successful marriage is to always be worthy of a temple recommend and to attend the temple frequently. Frequent temple attendance will help you remember who you are. Keeping the

> *"Marriage between a man and a woman is ordained of God."* – The Family: A Proclamation to the World

covenants you make in the temple will help you become the person your future spouse is looking for.

The Right Time

The right time to get married is different for everyone. There is no universal rule for when to get married, except to get married when you, your future spouse, and the Lord all know it is the right time. Elder Richard G. Scott married his sweetheart, Jeanine, two weeks after he returned from his mission. Sister Kristen Oaks had been home from her mission for thirty years when she married Elder Dallin H. Oaks.

Don't obsess. Don't postpone other aspects of your life to focus just on finding a spouse. Move forward with your life, make something of yourself, and become the kind of person your future spouse will want to marry. Build and nurture rewarding relationships. Continue with your education, and qualify yourself to earn a living. Continue to learn, progress, and achieve. After her mission, Sister Oaks earned her doctorate, had a successful career in educational publishing, and was a visiting assistant professor at Brigham Young University, all during the years she was single. That training and experience not only provided her with meaningful and rewarding employment but prepared her for assignments that she probably never dreamed of, including teaching and training auxiliary leaders in the Philippines during the two years that Elder Oaks served as the Area President there.

You don't need to obsess about getting married—as

important as it is, it is not the only focus of your life right now. You still need to focus on your education, think about your career, and serve in the Church. Dating and eventually marriage are an important part of the fabric of your life, but they are not the only part.

Don't delay. When you find the right person, don't delay marriage and children for selfish reasons. There is a marked tendency in society and in the Church to postpone adult responsibilities. Don't succumb to that trend. If you think you can't afford to get married, remember that your parents and grandparents didn't think they could afford it either. Be willing to postpone material comforts for the incomparable blessings of family.

> *"Some recently returned missionaries come home and have tunnel vision on the goal of getting married. That's all they think or talk about . . . Future marriage prospects tend to be more interested in somebody who continues their gospel study habits from the mission and who focuses on improving and excelling in all areas of life over somebody who can't think or talk about anything besides marriage."*
> *— A returned elder*

The Right Person

Finding the right person may appear daunting. It will be one of the great miracles of your life. Miracles happen when you pray fervently, exercise faith and good works, and follow the promptings of the Spirit. Like most of the miracles you experienced as a missionary, this one will happen in what appears to be a natural way.

Pray. Make finding your future husband or wife a matter of constant prayer. Pray about this every day. Commit to the Lord that you will be the husband and father or wife and mother that He expects you to be. Pray that you will meet the right person, then commit that you will always treat that person with love and kindness. Be specific: ask, "Should I marry [insert name]?" Pray to know with certainty, nothing doubting—this is the most important decision of your life. Pray to know, and have the faith to move forward. Keep praying until you get an answer.

> *"Believe that your faith has everything to do with your romance, because it does. You separate dating from discipleship at your peril." – Elder Jeffrey R. Holland, "How Do I Love Thee?"*

When you get that answer, be patient enough to allow that special person to get his or her own answer from God. When we were dating, Kathleen received a clear and certain witness that she was to marry Clark, and was a little disappointed when she saw him that evening and he didn't have that same knowledge. He was a little slower to get an answer, and she was patient

> *"The way to judge is as plain, that ye may know with a perfect knowledge, as the daylight is from the dark night." – Moroni 7:15; emphasis added*

enough not to say anything about what she already knew. Clark got his answer soon enough. Marrying each other was unquestionably the best thing we ever did!

Date. "Faith without works is dead" (James 2:26). One of your obligations is to actively socialize and date. This is sometimes easier for men than for women, but there is much that women can do to lead an active social life, including being approachable, available, friendly, and reciprocating friendship. In today's society, it is even acceptable for a woman to invite a man on a date.

Dating is different from just "hanging out." Elder Dallin H. Oaks noted, "Unlike hanging out, dating is not a team sport. Dating is pairing off to experience the kind of one-on-one association and temporary commitment that can lead to marriage."[1] You are at an age when it is time to begin looking seriously for a marriage partner, and that means you need to get to know some members of the opposite sex well. You'll never learn enough about each other by just hanging out in groups.

Elder Dallin H. Oaks, "Dating versus Hanging Out," *Ensign,* June 2006, http://www.lds.org/ensign/2006/06/dating-versus-hanging-out

Your responsibility is to be "anxiously engaged" (D&C 58:27) in finding a spouse, and dating is essential to fulfilling that responsibility.

Seek to know what is important and what isn't. When Clark was single and in graduate school, he made a list of the qualities he was looking for in a wife. It was a good idea but poorly executed. By this we mean that thinking about and even writing down what you are looking for in a spouse can be a helpful exercise as it forces you to articulate some of your hopes and dreams. But Clark's list was poorly conceived and written: when he first met Kathleen, she didn't seem to match up to his list. What he soon discovered was that he had the right girl and the wrong list. He saw in her qualities that he hadn't really thought much about and realized that most of the items on his list were superficial and unimportant. Kathleen had a similar experience when she met Clark, but she soon realized that he had qualities that were not on her list but that she desired in a mate.

Whether a woman has long hair and looks great without makeup or a man has thick hair and a muscular build probably doesn't matter too much in the long run. But how committed he or she is to the gospel, how kind, how thoughtful, how humble, and how obedient he or she is does make a difference. Find someone who loves the Lord even more than he or she loves you.

It Will All Work Out

In the end, your prayers and the answers you receive override all other considerations. Seek to know and do the Lord's will, and everything else will work out. Be willing to accept His timetable, even if it is different than what you want. Your choice of a mate is not just important to you, it is important to the Lord. He is as concerned about who you marry as you are. The Spirit will guide you in simple, sometimes almost imperceptible ways, just as it did when you were a missionary. You don't need to worry; you can be anxiously engaged in seeking marriage without being anxious. Be prayerful, be patient, "cheerfully do all things that lie in [your] power;

> *"If you do your best, it will all work out. Put your trust in God, and move forward with faith and confidence in the future."*
> *– President Gordon B. Hinckley,* Church News, *Oct. 4, 1997*

and then . . . stand still, with the utmost assurance, to see the salvation of God, and for his arm to be revealed" (D&C 123:17).

REMEMBER THIS

1. The most important thing you will ever do is to marry the right person in the right place at the right time.

2. Cheerfully do all that lies within your power, then leave the rest up to the Lord.

11

Hastening the Work

The knowledge and power of God are expanding;
The veil o'er the earth is beginning to burst.
Hymns, no. 2

When Jacob returned to his home in Florida following his mission, he was called as the ward mission leader. During the next year—his first year home from his mission—he participated in five convert baptisms, including one member of his extended family. It was a year of miracles that seamlessly followed the years of his mission.

Evan enrolled at Brigham Young University within a few weeks of his return from his mission. On one of his first Sundays in Provo, Utah, a beautiful fall day, he and his roommate decided to take a walk around campus and just enjoy the sunshine. They saw a young man walking towards them and, still in the habit of talking with everyone, Evan stopped and talked with the young man. Alfonso was from Peru and had been in Provo only a few days. He had come to study in BYU's English Learning Program. When Evan asked where he was living, he responded that his apartment had just fallen through, and he was scrambling to find housing. Evan and his roommate still had room for one more student in their apartment, and they invited Alfonso to come live with them. Alfonso moved in with Evan, responded to the invitation to meet with the missionaries, and a month later Evan had the privilege of baptizing his new friend.

Whether you live in Florida or on the BYU campus in Provo, Utah, there are missionary opportunities awaiting you!

You have returned home at a time in history when the work of salvation is going forward in a remarkable way. President Thomas S. Monson said, "Now is the time for members and missionaries to come together, to work together, to labor in the Lord's vineyard to bring souls unto Him. He has prepared the means for us to share the gospel in a multitude of ways, and He will assist us in our labors if we will act in faith to fulfill His work."[1]

The Lord still has many missionary miracles in store for you throughout your life. You have been released as a full-time missionary, but you have not been released as a missionary: "Membership in the Lord's Church means being called to be fully engaged in His work of salvation."[2]

"Hastening the Work of Salvation: Members and Missionaries," http://www.lds.org/training/wwlt/2013/hastening/members-and-missionaries

Always a Missionary

There are many ways you can continue to experience the joy of missionary work. It doesn't matter what your Church calling is; every member is a missionary and can be an effective one.

Pray. Pray for the missionaries. Pray by name for the missionaries in your ward. Pray by name for their investigators. Pray that the Lord will place people in your path and give you opportunities to invite others to hear the message of the gospel. Prayer was an essential element in the miracles of your mission. It will continue to be an essential element in the miracles yet to come.

> "Pray and look for opportunities to serve, help, and lift others." — Preach My Gospel, 169

Have faith that you can share the restored gospel. As you strengthen your faith and come to believe that the Lord is preparing people to receive the message of the gospel, those people "will be placed in your path—He will lead you to them or He will lead them to you."[3] It happened to you as a full-time missionary; it will happen to you throughout your life.

> "He will lead you to them or He will lead them to you." — Preach My Gospel, 155

Know your missionaries. Get to know the full-time missionaries assigned to your ward. Go out with them on visits from time to time as your schedule allows. Elder S. Gifford Nielsen invited members to "pray for the missionaries serving in your area and their investigators by name every day."[4] Your local missionaries are your best support and resource.

Elder S. Gifford Nielsen, "Hastening the Lord's Game Plan!" October 2013 general conference, https://www.lds.org/ensign /2013/11/saturday-afternoon-session /hastening-the-lords-game-plan

"Talk with everyone." Kathleen's parents, Owen and Darlene Hansen, are the best missionaries we know. They have invited hundreds of people to hear the missionaries, and many of those people have been baptized. When Owen was a bishop in Dallas, Texas, Darlene explained to the postman why they were receiving so many packages from Salt Lake City; later that postman and his wife served as ordinance workers in the Dallas Texas Temple. Owen goes to a new barber frequently, always hoping that the barber will be someone he can invite to learn more about the Church.

> *"Once we have realized that we succeed as member missionaries when we invite people to learn and accept the truth, much of the fear that kept us from sharing the gospel vanishes."*
> — *Clayton M. Christensen,* The Power of Everyday Missionaries, 24

Talk with everyone about the Church.[5] Use Mormon vocabulary in your conversations — often it will open up a conversation about the Church.

You are successful when you invite others. As a full-time missionary, not only did you invite others to hear the message of the gospel but you taught them the gospel. As a member, you have access to the full-time missionaries who can do the teaching — your primary job is to invite others to meet with the missionaries. You are successful as a member-missionary when you invite others. "The invitation is the mark of success, not whether people get baptized or become active in the Church."[6]

Stay in touch with those you taught in the mission. Continue to pray for those you saw baptized as well as those you taught who were not baptized. Near the end of his mission, Michael spoke to a young couple with their infant daughter in front of a department store in Sabadell, Spain. The couple invited the missionaries to come to their home and teach them. They were a wonderful family but declined to accept the invitation to prepare for baptism. Within a few months, Michael returned home, but he kept in touch with this family. When the infant daughter

> *"When you go home, do not forget those you have taught. At all times live worthy of their trust. Write them occasionally and encourage them to be faithful."* — Missionary Handbook, 37

was sixteen years old, her parents wanted her to be an exchange student in the United States, and they contacted Michael for some assistance. By then, Michael was the principal of a high school, helped them make the necessary arrangements, and agreed to have their daughter live with him and his family. Seventeen years after first meeting the missionaries on the sidewalk, the family was baptized. A year later they traveled to Utah where Michael was living and asked him to be a witness as their family was sealed in the Salt Lake Temple.

Of special concern are those you worked with on your mission who were baptized but have fallen into inactivity. You can continue to make a difference in their life. Email, texting, social media, Skype, and other electronic means make it easier than ever to stay in touch. You can use these innovations to bless the lives of others.

ACTIVITY

Prayerfully select two or three converts or investigators that you worked with on your mission, and send them a message of love and encouragement.

You spent the last eighteen months or two years eating, living, and breathing missionary work, and you saw great miracles. The good news is that your full-time mission was just the beginning of your lifelong mission: the best is yet to come!

Clayton M. Christensen, *The Power of Everyday Missionaries,* http://www.every daymissionaries.org

REMEMBER THIS

1. You have returned home in an era when there is a great hastening of the work of salvation.

2. The Lord still has many missionary miracles in store for you.

12

Becoming a Disciple of Christ

I'll be what you want me to be.
Hymns, no. 270

As a full-time missionary, you understood your purpose; you could — and did — recite your purpose from memory:

"Invite others to come unto Christ by helping them receive the restored gospel through faith in Jesus Christ and His Atonement, repentance, baptism, receiving the gift of the Holy Ghost, and enduring to the end."[1]

Your purpose gave direction and meaning to everything you did as a missionary. Its two action verbs — *invite* and *help* — made it clear what you were to do, and you spent all your time inviting others to come unto Christ and helping them develop the faith necessary to repent, enter into sacred ordinances, and remain true and faithful.

The missionary purpose is essentially a short statement of the gospel, or doctrine of Christ. This doctrine is stated on page 5 of *Preach My Gospel:*

"[Jesus Christ] came into the world to do His Father's will, and His Father sent Him into the world to be lifted up on the cross. By His Atonement and Resurrection, all men will be lifted up to stand before Christ to be judged of their works, whether they be good or evil. Those who exercise faith in Christ, repent of their sins, and are baptized in Christ's name can be sanctified by the Holy Ghost. If they endure to the end, they will stand spotless before Christ at the last day and will enter into the rest of the Lord. Christ will hold them guiltless before the Father. He will be their Mediator and Advocate."

That paragraph summarizes the doctrine taught by Jesus Christ in 3 Nephi 11 and 3 Nephi 27, by Nephi in 2 Nephi 31, and by the Prophet Joseph Smith in Articles of Faith 1:1–4. This doctrine is the core of all we do in the Church. According to *Handbook 2: Administering the Church,* the purpose of the Church is to "assist in [God's] work to bring to pass the salvation and exaltation of His children. The Church invites all to 'come unto Christ, and be perfected in him' (Moroni 10:32; see also D&C 20:59). The invitation to come unto Christ pertains to all who have lived, or will ever live, on the earth. . . . In fulfilling its purpose to help individuals and families qualify for exaltation, the Church focuses on divinely appointed responsibilities. These include helping members live the gospel of Jesus Christ, gathering Israel through missionary work, caring for the poor and needy, and enabling the salvation of the dead by building temples and performing vicarious ordinances."[2]

"The Purpose of the Church," *Handbook 2,* page 9, https://www.lds.org/handbook /handbook-2-administering-the-church /priesthood-principles?lang=eng#22

The purpose of the Church is also your purpose: it tells you what to do—invite others to come unto Christ by helping members (active and less active) live the gospel, doing missionary work, caring for the poor, and assisting in temple and family history work. Like your missionary purpose, it contains the action verbs *invite* and *help.*

And in addition to instructing you on what to *do,* this brief paragraph also describes what you should *be*—"perfected in him." The great invitation from the Savior is, "I would that ye should be perfect even as I, or your Father who is in

> *"Just as vital as what you do . . . is who you are."*
> —Preach My Gospel, *115*

heaven is perfect" (3 Nephi 12:48). Note that the four elements of the purpose of the Church—and therefore your purpose as a member—all focus on serving others: members, nonmembers, the poor, the dead. As we serve others, we become perfected ourselves.

What we *do* determines in large measure who we *are:* when we pay our tithes and offerings, we become less selfish and more compassionate; then as we become less selfish and more compassionate, our desire to pay our tithes and offerings increases. What we *do* is inextricably interwoven with who we *are*. As we do what Christ did and what He asks of us, we become more Christlike; and as we develop Christlike attributes, our desire to do His will increases.

You have come home from your mission a very different person from who you were when you left. God invested heavily in you when He trusted you to serve as a full-time missionary. You are a leader, "a chosen generation, a royal priesthood, an holy nation" (1 Peter 2:9). Only a tiny fraction of God's children on the earth have been given the experiences and the training that you received as a missionary. He expects you now to make a difference in the world, to consecrate all that you have or may yet have to the building up of the kingdom of God. He expects you to be different from others, to be "a peculiar people" (1 Peter 2:9); He expects you to be a true disciple of Christ and to be Christlike in attributes and actions.

ACTIVITY

Review *Preach My Gospel,* chapter 6, and consider how that information applies to your postmission life. Complete the Attribute Activity on page 126, substituting *life* for "mission," *disciple* for "missionary," and *commandments* for "mission rules." Consider completing the Attribute Activity on a regular basis.

The gospel of Jesus Christ is a plan that enables you to become a disciple. As you build faith through study, prayer, and attendance at Church meetings, your faith motivates you to repent. Your repentance is manifest and enlivened as you participate in priesthood ordinances, such as partaking of the sacrament. Keeping the promises you make through ordinances renews the gift of the Holy Ghost in your life (see D&C 20:77), and the promptings of the Holy Ghost in your life increase your faith, which leads to additional repentance, ordinances, and an enlarged presence of the Spirit in your life. This cycle—faith, repentance, ordinances, the gift of the Holy Ghost—leads you ever upward in a spiral of perfection. It leads to sacred temple ordinances, including the sacred sealing ordinance. As you endure to the end, you become a disciple of Christ, perfected in Him.

We are a covenant people. Your mission was an extremely important step in your lifelong quest to become a disciple of Christ. You prepared yourself before serving, developed faith, repented, and made and kept covenants in order to be worthy to serve. Your missionary name tag was a public declaration of your covenants. Instead of a plastic name tag worn over your clothing, his name is now written upon your heart and your countenance. You covenant weekly to "always remember him" (D&C 20:77). You have made sacred covenants in the temple, and you wear a reminder of those covenants at all times. Keeping your covenants, at all times and in all places, is the mark of a successful returned missionary.

Your full-time mission was unique in many ways—you will never have another period of time in your life in which you can focus so exclusively on inviting others to come unto Christ without having to concern yourself with family, finances, food, shelter, and other necessities. But in the most important ways, your full-time mission was only the beginning of greater things. "Have miracles ceased? Behold I say unto you, Nay; neither have angels ceased to minister unto the children of men" (Moroni 7:29).

Now that you have been released, you have graduated from one of the great learning experiences of your life. As you build on that foundation, the Lord will continue to use you to carry out his work in remarkable ways. Most of the great miracles you will see in your life are still in the future. The Lord will continue to use you to invite His children to come unto Christ, and you will witness miracles as you help others build faith and live the doctrine of Christ. "O be wise; what can I say more?" (Jacob 6:12). "Cheerfully do all things that lie in [your] power" (D&C 123:17) to keep the covenants you have made. Your lifelong work has just begun, and the best is yet to come.

REMEMBER THIS

1. Your purpose as a returned missionary is similar to your missionary purpose.

2. The Lord has prepared you through your missionary service to become a leader and example.

3. Your mission was only the beginning of your lifelong quest to help bring others to Christ.

4. Keep your covenants at all times and in all places.

Onward, ever onward, as we glory in his name;
Onward, ever onward, as we glory in his name;
Forward, pressing forward, as a triumph song we sing,
God our strength will be; press forward, ever,
Called to serve our King.

HYMNS, NO. 249

Ten Suggestions for Parents of Returned Missionaries

Returning home can be awkward and difficult for a missionary. It can also be awkward and difficult for the family and friends of the missionary. These ten simple suggestions can enable parents to ease the transition of a newly returned missionary, reconnect after a prolonged absence, and build stronger and deeper relationships. While these suggestions are directed specifically to parents of returning missionaries, many of them are applicable to other family members and friends.

1. Recognize that your missionary has changed and that your relationship with your child has changed. Missionaries may leave home as immature teenagers or college students, but they return as adults. Treat your missionary like an adult, not like the child who left home eighteen or twenty-four months ago. Your relationship with your missionary is now a relationship of adult to adult more than parent to child. Rather than providing your missionary with all he or she needs to live—housing, food, clothing, recreation, etc.—your role is to help your missionary become self-reliant. You are no longer in charge of your missionary's life; rather, you are a trusted and loving friend, advisor, mentor, and parent. You will still need to guide and encourage your missionary as he or she takes on the full responsibilities of adulthood. And if you are humble, there is much you can learn from your missionary

2. Let your missionary talk. Returned missionaries have just come home from a life-changing experience, and most people they talk to never go beyond asking, "So, how was your mission?" Returned missionaries often feel that no one really understands the magnitude and gravity of what they have experienced and how they have changed. They need to share their experiences, their feelings, and their thoughts. Ask good questions: What were some of the most important things you learned on your mission? What was your favorite area, and why? Who did you teach there? How did you find them? What were zone conferences like? How many zones did you have? What were your mission standards of excellence? Tell me about your mission president. Tell me about your companions. Share with me a recent miracle you experienced.

Let your missionary talk.

Some families schedule a family vacation as soon as their missionary returns. This can be a wonderful time to become reacquainted and reestablish family connections. If you are planning a family vacation, remember that your missionary may have been teaching and serving people who may never go to Disneyland or stay in a nice hotel, and few venues are more uncomfortable for a recently returned missionary than the beach. Go somewhere that you can be together as a family, play some games, take a walk, and talk. Use this as an opportunity to let your missionary download his or her experiences and feel that someone other than former missionary companions now understands what he or she has felt and experienced. Try to feel what your missionary has felt and is feeling.

3. Learn to speak your missionary's language. For the past eighteen or twenty-four months your missionary studied *Preach My Gospel* every day. If you know the language of *Preach My Gospel*, you know your missionary's language. When you use language from *Preach My Gospel*, he or she understands you. When you use such terms as "set goals and make plans," "your purpose," and "the doctrine of Christ," your missionary understands you. You don't need to learn Spanish or Portuguese or Thai—if you can speak *Preach My Gospel*, you can communicate!

4. Don't rush your missionary's transition. Recently returned missionaries will feel awkward, especially in social situations. Your missionary will feel a little lost without the structure of the missionary schedule. Your missionary may want to put on missionary attire every morning (those *are* his or her comfortable clothes), study the scriptures for two hours each day, and attend the temple multiple times each week. Isn't that what you hoped for before he or she left?

Support your missionary in keeping the same standards

he or she kept as a missionary—getting up early, having personal prayer, studying the scriptures—and include your missionary in regular family prayer, family scripture study, and family home evening.

Help your missionary get some new clothes, but remember that he or she doesn't need a two-year wardrobe or trendy clothes. Start small. Encourage your missionary to have the demeanor of a returned missionary, to dress and groom like a returned missionary, to act like a returned missionary, to keep that returned missionary glow.

Let your missionary live a missionary schedule for as long as possible until other obligations require more of his or her time. Savor these precious moments as you savor the first few days after bringing a newborn home from the hospital. You don't need to rush your missionary into a new schedule; he or she will get into a new routine soon enough. Your missionary doesn't want to be "normal," and you don't want your missionary to be "normal"—he or she is a returned missionary, and we are, after all, a peculiar people. There are plenty of people out there who will urge your missionary to revert to who he or she once was—friends who didn't serve missions, friends who didn't change as much over the past two years, even family members. Encourage your missionary to remain extraordinary.

5. Help your missionary stay busy and productive. Missionaries are used to being fully engaged and occupied from 6:30 A.M. until 10:30 P.M., and they are happier when they are busy. Your missionary will be tired when he or she arrives home—exhausted physically and emotionally; help him or her get a couple of good nights' sleep, recover from jet lag, and then get busy. In the critical gap between your missionary's release by the stake president and beginning a job or school, help your missionary find worthwhile things to do. He or she is accustomed to serving others—help him or her find service opportunities in the family, the ward, and the community. Encourage your missionary to attend the temple, go out with the missionaries, or do family history work. Your missionary may need a few days' rest, but hard work is immensely satisfying, and service refines us and brings us happiness.

6. Let your missionary be a responsible adult. In the mission field your missionary did his or her own budgeting, shopping, housecleaning, and laundry, and took care of medical needs. Your missionary is used to setting goals and making plans, but life was so much simpler in the mission field. Your missionary will need your gentle guidance and support as he or she moves forward with life. Allow your missionary to make arrangements for medical and dental checkups. Ask about his or her plans for school and work. Provide encouragement but not pressure.

7. Encourage your missionary to seek a Church calling immediately. Returned missionaries don't need a break from serving. It's perfectly acceptable for them to ask the bishop for a calling right away. If your missionary doesn't receive a calling in a couple of weeks, consider approaching the bishop yourself. If you live near a temple, encourage your missionary to become a temple worker. Your missionary's bishop needs to make the recommendation and endorsement, but it is a calling that does not require any adjustment in the ward organization, and it is an extremely rewarding calling for a newly returned missionary. Remember that returned missionaries have been entrusted to gather God's children and declare the gospel of repentance, many of them have conducted worthiness interviews, and some have served as leaders and even branch presidents. Your missionary is experienced and capable, and he or she needs to continue working in the kingdom. The sooner returned missionaries lose themselves again in service, the sooner they will find their way in their new stage of life.

8. Encourage your missionary to select a ward and get involved. Many young single adults have the option to be members of a Young Single Adult Ward or to remain in a conventional ward. You may want your missionary with you in Church meetings for the first couple of weeks, and he or she will probably be more comfortable attending with family, but then your missionary needs to make a decision and stick with it. Sometimes returned missionaries will attend a conventional ward for a few weeks, then attend the YSA ward, then try another YSA ward. Encourage your returned missionary to stay in one ward, accept a calling, develop a relationship with priesthood and auxiliary leaders, and build friendships.

9. Help your missionary set goals, make plans, and carry out those plans. In the mission field missionaries practiced the skills of setting goals, making plans, and carrying out those plans (see *Preach My Gospel*, 137–54), but many returned missionaries struggle to apply those skills in a much more complex environment that includes education, career choices, social life, dating, marriage, etc. Ask your missionary good questions, and encourage and discuss various alternatives. If your missionary is having trouble setting big goals—what to major in, what career to pursue—help him or her focus on smaller goals until the bigger ones become clear. But ultimately, having goals and working towards them will propel your missionary forward in life; the absence of goals can result in a great deal of wasted time and effort (see *Preach My Gospel*, 146).

10. Help your missionary understand that the best is yet to come. Not all missionaries are happy to be home—they loved their mission and hated to see it end. It really was the best eighteen months or two years of their life, and they sometimes feel that the best of their life is now over. Help your missionary understand that the mission was only the best years of his or her life *so far*. Help your missionary understand that the best things in life still lie ahead and that the mission has prepared him or her for even greater and more rewarding experiences yet to come.

Notes

Epigraph, page v: Perry, "Let Him Do It with Simplicity," 7.

Introduction

1. Scott, "Power of *Preach My Gospel*," 31.
2. Perry, "Returned Missionary," 77.

Chapter 2: Is It "A Hard Thing?"

1. Novotny et al., "Pessimistic Explanatory Style Is Prognostic," 326.
2. Andersen, "It's a Miracle," 78.

Chapter 3: "Mind the Gap"

1. Kiskaddon, "The Time to Decide," in *Rhymes of the Ranges*, 108–9.
2. Monson, "Be of Good Cheer," 92.

Chapter 4: Getting Started

1. Perry, "Returned Missionary," 77.
2. Churchill, "Never Give In." Churchill's actual admonition

was as follows: "Never give in, never give in, never, never, never—in nothing great or small, large or petty—never give in except to conviction of honour and good sense."

Chapter 5: The Cornerstones of a Successful Transition

1. Pinnock, "Learning Our Father's Will," 75.

2. Scott, "Acquiring Spiritual Knowledge," 86.

3. Hinckley, *Preach My Gospel*, 108.

4. *Preach My Gospel*, 89.

5. *Brigham Young* [manual], 68.

Chapter 7: How to Write Your Own Handbook

1. *Missionary Handbook*, 1.

2. *Missionary Handbook*, 10–11.

3. Rector, "Live above the Law to Be Free," 131.

4. Perry, "Returned Missionary," 77.

5. Holland, "'This Do in Remembrance of Me,'" 68.

6. *For the Strength of Youth*, 11.

7. *For the Strength of Youth*, 12.

8. See Bushman, "Do Violent Video Games Increase Aggression?"

9. Packer, Word of Wisdom," 18.

10. Ashton, *One for the Money*, 6.

11. *For the Strength of Youth*, 35.

12. *For the Strength of Youth*, 36.

13. *For the Strength of Youth*, 36.

14. Bednar, "To Sweep the Earth As with a Flood."

Chapter 8: "Set Goals and Make Plans"

1. Brady, *Goal Oriented Life*, 1.

2. *Teachings of Thomas S. Monson*, 123.

3. *Preach My Gospel*, 146.

4. *Teachings of Thomas S. Monson*, 124.

Chapter 9: The Importance of Education

1. *Teachings of Gordon B. Hinckley*, 167–73.
2. *Joseph Fielding Smith* [manual], 141.
3. *Teachings of Thomas S. Monson*, 95.
4. *For the Strength of Youth*, 9.
5. *For the Strength of Youth*, 9.
6. *Brigham Young* [manual], 197.
7. *Teachings of Gordon B. Hinckley*, 172.
8. *Teachings of Thomas S. Monson*, 96.
9. *Brigham Young* [manual], 197.
10. *Brigham Young* [manual], 196.
11. Uchtdorf, "Two Principles for Any Economy," 58; Articles of Faith 1:13.
12. *Joseph Fielding Smith* [manual], 142.
13. Uchtdorf, "Two Principles for Any Economy," 58.
14. McConkie, "Obedience, Consecration and Sacrifice," 51.

Chapter 10: Dating and Marriage

1. Oaks, "Dating versus Hanging Out," 12.

Chapter 11: Hastening the Work

1. Monson, "Faith in the Work of Salvation."
2. "Hastening the Work of Salvation," 37.
3. *Preach My Gospel*, 169, 155.
4. Nielsen, "Hastening the Lord's Game Plan," 34.
5. *Preach My Gospel*, 169.
6. "Hastening the Work of Salvation," 39.

Chapter 12: Becoming a Disciple of Christ

1. *Preach My Gospel*, 1.
2. *Handbook 2*, 9.

Sources

Andersen, Neil L. "It's a Miracle." *Ensign*, May 2013, 77–80.

Ashton, Marvin H. *One for the Money: Guide to Family Finances.* Salt Lake City: The Church of Jesus Christ of Latter-day Saints, 2006.

Bednar, David A. "To Sweep the Earth As with a Flood." Address delivered Aug. 29, 2014, Brigham Young University, Provo, Utah. https://www.lds.org/prophets-and-apostles/unto -all-the-world/to-sweep-the-earth-as-with-a-flood.

Brady, Rodney H. *A Goal Oriented Life Is Far More Likely to Lead to Success Than Is a Life That Leaves Success to Chance.* http://media .bonnint.net/bonnint/0/1/123.pdf.

Bushman, Brad J. "Do Violent Video Games Increase Aggression?" *Psychology Today.* http://www.psychologytoday.com/blog /get-psyched/201201/do-violent-video-games-increase -aggression.

Christensen, Clayton M. *The Power of Everyday Missionaries: The What and How of Sharing the Gospel.* Salt Lake City: Deseret Book, 2013. http://www.everydaymissionaries.org.

Churchill, Winston. "Never Give In." Address delivered Oct. 29, 1941, at Harrow, London. http://www.winstonchurchill .org/learn/speeches/speeches-of-winston-churchill/103 -never-give-in.

"Education." *Gospel Topics.* https://www.lds.org/topics /education.

The Family: A Proclamation to the World. Salt Lake City: The Church of Jesus Christ of Latter-day Saints, 1997.

For the Strength of Youth. Salt Lake City: The Church of Jesus Christ of Latter-day Saints, 2011.

Handbook 2: Administering the Church. Salt Lake City: The Church of Jesus Christ of Latter-day Saints, 2010.

"Hastening the Work of Salvation." *Ensign,* Oct. 2013, 36–39.

"Hastening the Work of Salvation: Members and Missionaries." https://www.lds.org/training/wwlt/2013/hastening /members-and-missionaries.

Hinckley, Clark B. "Five Questions to Ask Before You Click 'Post,'" *The Best Is Yet to Come* (blog). http://brillanrayos .blogspot.com/2014/02/five-questions-to-ask-before-you -click.html.

Hinckley, Gordon B. "Messages of Inspiration from President Hinckley." *LDS Church News,* Oct. 4, 1997. http://www.lds churchnewsarchive.com/articles/29119/Messages-of -inspiration-from-President-Hinckley.html.

———. "Power of the Book of Mormon." *Ensign,* June 1988, 2–6.

———. *Teachings of Gordon B. Hinckley.* Salt Lake City: Deseret Book, 1997.

Holland, Jeffrey R. *"How Do I Love Thee?"* Address delivered Feb. 15, 2000, at Brigham Young University, Provo, Utah.

———. "Like a Broken Vessel." *Ensign,* Nov. 2013, 40–42.

———. "Safety for the Soul." *Ensign,* Nov. 2009, 88–90.

———. "'This Do in Remembrance of Me.'" *Ensign,* Nov. 1995, 67–69.

Hymns of The Church of Jesus Christ of Latter-day Saints. Salt Lake City: The Church of Jesus Christ of Latter-day Saints, 1985.

Kiser, G. Craig. "A Principle with Promises." *Ensign,* Feb. 2014, 72–74.

Kiskaddon, Bruce. "The Time to Decide." In *Rhymes of the Ranges: A New Collection of the Poems of Bruce Kiskaddon,* 108–9. Layton, Utah: Gibbs Smith, 1987.

Kopischke, Erich W. "Being Accepted of the Lord." *Ensign,* May 2013, 104–6.

McConkie, Bruce R. "Obedience, Consecration and Sacrifice." *Ensign,* May 1975, 50–52.

Missionary Handbook. Salt Lake City: The Church of Jesus Christ of Latter-day Saints, 2006.

Monson, Thomas S. "Be of Good Cheer." *Ensign,* May 2009, 89–92.

———. "Faith in the Work of Salvation." Worldwide Leadership Training broadcast, 2013. https://www.lds.org/broadcasts /article/worldwide-leadership-training/2013/06/faith-in -the-work-of-salvation?lang=eng

———. *Teachings of Thomas S. Monson.* Salt Lake City: Deseret Book, 2011.

Nielsen, S. Gifford. "Hastening the Lord's Game Plan!" *Ensign,* Nov. 2013, 33–35.

Novotny, Paul, et al. "A Pessimistic Explanatory Style Is Prognostic for Poor Lung Cancer Survival." *Journal of Thoracic Oncology* 5, no. 3 (Mar. 2010): 326–32.

Oaks, Dallin H. "Dating versus Hanging Out." *Ensign,* June 2006, 10–16.

Packer, Boyd K. "The Word of Wisdom: The Principle and the Promises." *Ensign,* May 1996, 17–19.

"Patriarchal Blessings: Video." *Gospel Topics*. http://www.lds
.org/topics/patriarchal-blessings/video-audio.

Perry, L. Tom. "Let Him Do It with Simplicity." *Ensign*, Nov. 2008,
7–10.

———. "The Returned Missionary." *Ensign*, Nov. 2001, 75–77.

Pinnock, Hugh W. "Learning Our Father's Will." *Ensign*, Nov.
1984, 73–75.

Preach My Gospel. Salt Lake City: The Church of Jesus Christ of
Latter-day Saints, 2004.

Rector, Hartman, Jr. "Live above the Law to Be Free." *Ensign*, Jan.
1973, 130–31.

Scott, Richard G. "Acquiring Spiritual Knowledge." *Ensign*, Nov.
1993, 86–88.

———. "The Power of *Preach My Gospel*." *Ensign*, May 2005, 29–31.

Smith, Joseph Fielding. *Joseph Fielding Smith* [manual]. Teachings
of Presidents of the Church series. Salt Lake City: The Church
of Jesus Christ of Latter-day Saints, 2013.

Uchtdorf, Dieter F. "Two Principles for Any Economy." *Ensign*,
Nov. 2009, 55–58.

Wilcox, Brad. "Why Write It?" *Ensign*, Sept. 1999, 56–57.

Young, Brigham. *Brigham Young* [manual]. Teachings of Presidents
of the Church series. Salt Lake City: The Church of Jesus
Christ of Latter-day Saints, 1977.

Index

About the Authors

Clark and Kathleen Hinckley first met in the foyer of the Longfellow Park chapel in Cambridge, Massachusetts, in February of 1973; they were married the following October in the Salt Lake Temple. They have six children and nineteen grandchildren. They have lived in New York City, Michigan, and Arizona, and currently reside in Salt Lake City.

Both Clark and Kathleen are graduates of Brigham Young University. Clark also earned a master's degree in business administration (MBA) from the Harvard Business School.

Kathleen's address "The Power of a Holy Woman" was published in *Continue Your Journey and Let Your Hearts Rejoice: Talks from the 2013 BYU Women's Conference*. Clark is the author of *Christopher Columbus: "A Man among the Gentiles."*

Clark served a mission in Argentina as a young man and presided over the Spain Barcelona Mission from 2009 to 2012 with Kathleen as his companion. Clark has been a bishop and a stake president; Kathleen has served in ward and stake auxiliary presidencies. They currently serve as temple workers.